Efficiency Wages

Efficiency Wages
Models of Unemployment, Layoffs, and Wage Dispersion

Andrew Weiss

Princeton University Press
Princeton, New Jersey

To Bonnie, Annie, Kara, and Judith
who gave me the time to write
during "vacations."

Copyright © 1990 by Princeton University Press
Published by Princeton University Press, 41 William Street, Princeton, New Jersey 08540

Library of Congress Cataloging-in-Publication Data

Weiss, Andrew
    Efficiency wages : models of unemployment, layoffs, and wage dispersion / Andrew
Weiss.
    p. cm.
    Includes bibliographical references and index.
    ISBN 0-691-04279-9 (alk. paper)—ISBN 0-691-00388-2 (pbk. : alk. paper).
    1. Wages.   2. Incentives in industry.   3. Unemployment.
I. Title.
HD4909.W46 1990b
331.2'164—dc20   90–45925

Princeton University Press books are printed on acid-free paper, and meet the guidelines for
permanence and durability of the Committee on Production Guidelines for Book Longevity
of the Council on Library Resources

Printed in the United States of America by Princeton University Press,
Princeton, New Jersey

10 9 8 7 6 5 4 3 2 1

10 9 8 7 6 5 4 3 2 1
(Pbk.)

Contents

Preface

This monograph is intended both to provide an overview of the principal efficiency wage models and to present some new results in the field. The mathematics have been intentionally de-emphasized so as to make the material accessible to advanced undergraduates. All of the results are explained verbally and most are motivated through specific numerical examples.

Part I is concerned with the sorting effects of wages, or more generally wage schedules, in an economy where workers have information about their own productivity that is not available to firms. Part II is concerned with the direct effects of wages and wage schedules on the performance of workers. In Part II we assume that workers have no private information about their own productivity. The two parts may be read independently. Section 1, which appears before Part I, addresses some of the criticisms that have been made of efficiency wage models. The material in this section is relevant to both parts of the monograph.

Christophe Chamley, Gerhard Clemenz, Jean-Michel Grandmont, Kevin Lang, and Ruqu Wang have all made valuable suggestions for improving the exposition. Of course, any remaining errors or ambiguities are my responsibility. I am grateful to Andrea Borja and Ruqu Wang for valuable research assistance, and to Joyce Smith for her help in preparing the monograph.

Efficiency Wages
Models of Unemployment, Layoffs and Wage Dispersion

ANDREW WEISS

Department of Economics, Boston University, MA, USA

1. INTRODUCTION AND OVERVIEW

In discussing models of long-term unemployment we are motivated by the question "If a firm faces an excess supply of labor why doesn't it cut its wages?" This is a somewhat different question than the usual macro-economic question concerning insufficient aggregate demand. Here we are simply asking, regardless of the level of aggregate demand, why don't markets clear at the micro-economic level? Firms are presumably maximizing their profits. In the conventional micro-economic analysis whatever the level of aggregate demand firms would offer the lowest wage that would satisfy their labor demand. Consequently, as Modigliani pointed out, downward wage rigidity is necessary for an unemployment equilibrium.

Several reasons have been offered for downward wage rigidity. Azariadis [1975], Gordon [1974], and Baily [1974] presented implicit contract models in which they argued that risk aversion by workers would induce firms to offer a fixed wage contract. However, in these models the level of employment is above the level achieved in a Walrasian equilibrium. This is because risk neutral firms would wish to insure workers not just against wage fluctuations, but also against the income fluctuations associated with unemployment. If, as is commonly assumed in the implicit contract literature, a firm cannot commit itself to future wage payments to workers that it no longer employs, then the only way firms can lower the variance of their workers earnings is by employing them in states in which the value of their output is less than their private value of leisure (including the unemployment benefits they receive). On the other hand, if workers could be paid when not employed, the equilibrium contracts would leave workers indifferent

1

between being employed and unemployed.[1] These issues are discussed by Russell Cooper [1987] in his survey of the literature on implicit contracts and will not concern us any further.

The other leading explanations for downward wage rigidity are based on the effect of wage contracts on the quality of labor. In these efficiency wage models, wages affect the quality of labor either through their effect on the distribution of workers hired—the adverse selection effect; or through their effect on the performance of individual workers—the incentive effect.

The basic presumption of these models is that the labor market is substantively different from the model of product markets discussed in the typical elementary economics texts. In those models it is typically assumed that both buyers and sellers act as price takers. Although in most product markets prices affect the distribution of buyers and sellers as well as their behavior, it is usually reasonable to assume that neither buyers nor sellers care about how price changes affect the unobserved characteristics of their trading partners nor how their product will be used.[2] In the typical model of a product market, if the market clears at a given price no buyer would offer to pay a higher price. For example, in the Ricardian model as the price of wheat falls, low productivity land is taken out of production. However, buyers of wheat are unconcerned whether they are buying wheat that was grown on high or low productivity land. This is because the unobservable characteristics of wheat that are correlated with the quality of land on which it was grown are not sufficiently important to negate the conventional Walrasian analysis.

In the labor market, buyers of labor services are faced with considerable uncertainty concerning many aspects of the productivity of the workers they are hiring. *If lowering the wage they offer significantly lowers the average ability of the job applicants they face, firms may find that lowering their wage makes them worse off.* The adverse

---

[1] In the implicit contracting literature there is homogeneous labor, and effort is exogenously given; thus the only reason for inefficiencies in the allocation of labor stem from imperfect attempts at risk sharing between workers and firms.

[2] We are assuming that goods are paid for when they are purchased. If sellers extend credit to buyers the adverse selection and incentive effects of prices again become important. (See Gerhard Clemenz [1986] for a useful survey of the effects of imperfect information on credit contracts.)

selection aspect of labor markets is an essential feature of those markets while it is often of only secondary importance in product markets.[3]

In labor markets (or credit or product markets) in which informational asymmetries are important there may be too little (or no) trade because of the adverse selection effect of wages. A rigorous analysis of markets with important informational asymmetries in which unobserved characteristics are correlated with the reservation price (wage) of sellers shows that the Walrasian market-clearing price may not be consistent with optimizing behavior by agents. Thus defining an equilibrium as a set of prices at which markets clear is inappropriate. It is possible that no firms would choose to charge the market clearing price, and if it were chosen by all firms, one firm could increase its profits by deviating from the Walrasian price.

While adverse selection models of the labor market are motivated by a concern with unobserved differences among workers, these models should not be thought of as only relevant to young workers. The important feature of these models is informational asymmetries. Riordan and Staiger [1987] have presented a model of the labor market in which employers are better informed about the characteristics of their workers than are other firms. In that model adverse selection considerations coupled with sectoral shocks generate unemployment, because firms do not wish to hire the laid off workers in sectors suffering negative demand shocks. Indeed, one could argue that informational asymmetries become more marked as workers gain experience with particular firms, and thus that adverse selection considerations are even more important for older workers than for younger ones.

---

[3] Similarly, adverse selection or sorting considerations may be of great importance in credit and equity markets. The joke about the banker who "would never lend to anyone willing to pay his interest rates" plays on our understanding that the adverse selection effect of high interest rates is outweighing the direct effect of those interest rates on bank profits. Because of the adverse selection effects of interest rates and collateral requirements, the market equilibrium may be characterized by loan contracts and interest rates offered to depositors that together generate an excess demand for loans. Banks do not respond to this excess demand by raising the interest rate they charge because of the adverse selection consequences of higher interest rates would lower their profits. Indeed, there may not exist a profitable interest rate on loans (see Stiglitz and Weiss [1981, 1983]). Similarly in the used car market, as buyers lower the price they offer for cars the distribution of cars they are offered may deteriorate. The market equilibrium may be characterized by an excess supply of cars being offered for sale and by too little trade taking place. (See Akerlof [1970] and Wilson [1979]).

Wages (and prices) also affect behavior. These effects are both direct and indirect. The most direct effect of wages on behavior is on nutrition. In less developed countries the wages of workers directly affect their health, mental alertness, and physical well being. These effects are not limited to wages that are below the level needed to satisfy the worker's caloric requirements for the job. Workers, even at very low wages, will use some of their income to support family members and for consumption of goods and services other than food, shelter and medical care. Consequently there may be a significant range of wages at which increasing the wage increases the labor endowment of the worker through improved nutrition and health care. Indeed, the prevalence of subsidized meals, housing and medical care in the industrial sector of less developed countries suggests the importance of these effects. These direct effects of wages on worker productivity have been modeled by Leibenstein [1957], Bliss and Stern [1978a, b] and Dasgupta and Ray [1986, 1987].

The first models of the indirect effect of wages on worker productivity investigated the effect of wages on quit propensity (see Hammermesh and Goldfarb [1970], Salop [1973a, b], and Stiglitz [1974b]). Firms for which quits are costly are reluctant to cut wages when faced with an excess supply of workers. Lowering their wages would increase their turnover costs. Of course, the firm could lower the wage it pays newly hired workers while maintaining high wages for previously hired workers. However, multi-tiered wage structures of that form often generate serious morale problems.[4] To the extent that newly hired and experienced workers need to co-operate, the frictions caused by a multi-

---

[4] The July 29, 1987 issue of the *New York Times* reports that the low wage workers in two tier wage schemes fail to co-operate with their higher paid co-workers, frequently give poorer service to customers, and generally have lower productivity. These reports claim that the low productivity of the lower paid workers is due to the disparity in pay between the low paid workers and their higher paid co-workers. The low productivity of low paid workers could, of course, be due to either the sorting or incentive effects of wages and have nothing to do with the higher pay received by their co-workers.

Lindbeck and Snower [1984–1988] present models of the effects of differential treatment of newly hired and experienced workers. The Lindbeck and Snower models assume that the experienced workers will fail to co-operate with the less experienced workers. It would appear that the main results of their model would hold, if it were the low paid workers that failed to co-operate with the higher paid workers. In either case, firms would not necessarily wish to replace experienced workers with lower paid inexperienced ones.

tiered wage structure could impose serious costs on the firm. Note that we are not arguing against firms reducing quits by paying wages that rise steeply with tenure. Rather we are arguing against models in which firms respond to job queues by lowering the expected life-time wage of newly hired workers.

Analyses of the effect of wages on quits differ markedly from analyses of the direct effect of wages on nutrition. Quits are affected not only by the wage contract the worker is receiving, but also by the wages and hiring rates of the other firms in the economy as well as the unemployment rate. The unemployment rate affects the responsiveness of quits to changes in a firm's wage offer even if quits do not involve intervening spells of unemployment. This is because the unemployment rate affects the ratio of applicants to vacancies at different wages, and hence the probability of a worker receiving a wage offer above his current wage.

In addition to their effect on quits and nutrition, wages also affect effort. If workers were to receive wages that make them indifferent between staying with the firm and becoming unemployed, workers would always choose the levels of effort they find most enjoyable or least onerous. Neither the threat of being fired nor the threat of a wage cut would induce a higher level of effort: Since the worker would be indifferent between employment and unemployment, being fired is not a punishment. Similarly, since the worker would respond to a wage cut by quitting the firm or shirking (quitting on the job), wage cuts would have no incentive effects. The lower the wage, the more resources the firm would have to expend on supervision to maintain a given level of effort from its workers. In the limit, if the wage made workers indifferent between working and unemployment, the firm would have to constantly monitor each worker.

The effect of wages on effort depends on the expected utility from being unemployed and the degree of monitoring chosen by firms. The expected utility from unemployment depends, in turn, on the joint distribution of wage offers, the arrival times of those wage offers for an unemployed worker, and the expected duration of employment at each new job, as well as the worker's income while unemployed and his value of leisure. In particular, if no firms were hiring workers who had previously been fired for low effort then obviously the utility of unemployment would be independent of the wages offered to new entrants and the unemployment rate.

1.1. Criticisms of efficiency wage models

Readers who have no previous acquaintance with efficiency wage
models may wish to skip this section and return to it after familiarizing
themselves with some of the models presented in Sections 2–8.

If equilibrium is characterized by job queues, one question that
naturally arises is why firms don't "sell" jobs either by requiring lump
sum payments from newly hired workers, or requiring those workers
to work at low wages during some initial "apprenticeship" period.
Carmichael [1985] emphasizes that, although capital market imperfections prevent workers from being able to pay a bond that equals the
monetary value of the surplus they will gain from the job, if workers are
sufficiently risk averse, they can be charged fees that are large enough
to make them indifferent between employment and unemployment.
Alternatively workers can be initially assigned to low wage jobs at
which, even if effort were not monitored, the workers would be contributing some profit to the firm. These low wage job assignments
would be long enough to eliminate the surplus accruing to the worker
from his eventual employment at the high wage job. By having these
payments made by newly hired workers, the firm is still able to have low
quit rates and high levels of effort by paying high wages to experienced
workers. Thus Carmichael argues that the need to pay high wages to
experienced workers does not prevent firms from capturing the associated surplus, thereby eliminated job queues.

There are several problems with this critique of efficiency wage
models. First it does not apply to the adverse selection or nutrition
models.[5] For those models, requiring workers to buy their jobs would

---

[5] For certain parameter values, involuntary unemployment that is sustained by adverse
selection considerations could be eliminated by contracts that combine a low wage
apprenticeship program with tests. In that more sophisticated version of the adverse
selection model workers are tested at the end of their low wage apprenticeship program.
Their wage is a function of their score on the test. Consequently only workers that believe
they will do well on the test will apply for firms offering this apprenticeship-test contract.
If the cost of sorting workers through this apprenticeship-testing program is sufficiently
low, and some other more technical conditions are satisfied, these apprenticeship-testing
contracts can eliminate unemployment equilibria in the adverse selection model. An alternative means of eliminating unemployment in the adverse selection model is to have
workers compete for jobs through their level of schooling. There may be a large social
cost associated with alleviating the "involuntary" nature of the unemployment, by
having workers stay in school merely as a means of competing for jobs. In this case the
unemployed are workers with the lowest levels of education. Formally this unemployment is voluntary since they could become employed by choosing to go to school longer.
However, as in the case of low wage apprenticeships in the effort model, these semantic
distinctions seem more likely to obfuscate than illuminate the issues that concern us.

negatively affect the expected productivity of the firm's work force in much the same way as would offering low lifetime wages. Thus the Carmichael critique is not valid if firms are offering high wages as a means of improving the quality of their applicant pool or as a means of directly improving the fitness of their workers. Similarly the Carmichael critique is irrelevant if high wages are paid for their morale enhancing effects or to generate good will among the firm's workers.

Second, the elimination of unemployment by having workers "suffer" (either by accepting low initial wealth or low initial wages) does not eliminate and may aggravate the social problems normally associated with unemployment. Although the level of suffering required to get a job makes the marginal worker indifferent between working and not working, there are many workers that are made strictly better off by being able to buy a job, rather than facing a lottery. These will, in general, be workers with large wealth holdings or rich parents for whom the cost of buying a job has a small effect on their consumption during that initial period. Thus the allocation of jobs and of lifetime income may be less equitable than in the pure efficiency wage model with random job allocations.

Third, because capital markets are imperfect, forcing workers to buy jobs by working at low wages when they are young imposes large social costs. These costs are due to the same informational asymmetries that cause unemployment in the efficiency wage—effort models when workers cannot buy jobs. Indeed the notion that involuntary unemployment is eliminated by having workers buy their jobs by working at low wages for long periods does not seem to be a very useful way to frame the issues. An individual that is being paid close to zero, is contributing almost no effort and is indifferent between working and staying home (as in the Akerlof and Katz model) may be labeled as employed, but that labeling will tend to cloud our understanding of the effects of information asymmetries on labor markets. Whether the incentive effects of wages result in unemployment or in long periods of low wage employment during which effort levels are low, the associated social and economic problems are likely to be similar.[6]

---

[6] Many of these low wage apprenticeship programs and lump sum transfer schemes have been criticized as giving firms the possibility of absconding with the money. Akerlof and Katz get around this problem for low wage apprenticeship programs by letting firm specific human capital increase with job tenure. An alternative method would be for workers to be promised pensions, where the pensions are set aside for the workers. However, laws requiring full vesting after ten years of employment, and imperfections in capital markets reduce the usefulness of such schemes.

Finally, although contracts that require workers to buy their jobs by working at very low wages during some initial (possibly lengthy) period of employment eliminate so-called involuntary unemployment, the level of employment is below that which would maximize output or social welfare.

On the other hand, in the effort inducing version of the efficiency wage model, requiring workers to buy their jobs, could result in an efficient level of employment being achieved. This would be the case if workers are risk neutral and had sufficient wealth to pay firms the expected value of the surplus they will receive from future employment. Of course, workers are not risk neutral and do not have unlimited wealth, but the question might still be asked as to whether outside financing of performance bonds would generate the same result. The answer is no! The same informational asymmetries that give rise to efficiency wages being offered, combined with the possibility of personal bankruptcy, will deter bank financing of performance bonds.

To see this, suppose a bank were to finance a performance bond. Then in states in which the borrower is employed, the value of the job is decreased by the interest the borrower must pay the bank as a financing charge for the bond. In states in which the worker is unemployed, the worker declares bankruptcy and defaults on the bond. Consequently, if bankruptcy is permitted the penalty for being fired might be smaller with bank financed performance bonds than without them: the fired worker loses his wage, but also no longer has to pay the finance charges on the performance bond.

If workers default when fired, not only do bank financed performance bonds *accentuate* the incentive and adverse selection problems described above, but banks are unlikely to finance performance bonds for workers. (Usually discussions of performance bonds implicitly assume that these bonds are self financed, or that personal bankruptcy is not permitted.)

In contrast to the effort models, in the typical quit models, where workers are risk neutral and all quits are associated with job changes, bank financed performance bonds do not affect behavior, even if bankruptcy is not permitted. The performance bond serves as a lump sum cost. Workers still seek to maximize their life-time income.

On the other hand, if some quits are quits into unemployment, a bank financed performance bond would increase the probability of a worker quitting. To see this consider a long spell of unemployment. The borrower will not pay the interest on the loan. Thus in some unemployment states the loss of income from being unemployed is partially offset from the savings gained from no longer paying interest on the bank debt. Hence quits into unemployment are made more attractive.

Similarly, in the Guasch and Weiss [1980a, 1982]) adverse selection models, banks would not give loans to finance performance bonds. In those models the performance bonds are combined with imprecise, but accurate, tests to sort borrowers. Each borrower takes into account his probability of passing a firm's test as well as the wages offered conditional of passing or failing the test in choosing which firm(s) to apply to. Bank financed performance bonds would induce borrowers to apply for jobs with firms at which their probability of being successful is low, but the wage conditional on success is high. This is because the application fees are only fully repaid if the worker is successful. By applying to firms where his probability of success is low the worker effectively reduces the expected cost of the bank loan.[7] Knowing this, banks would not finance performance bonds nor would they make loans that enabled workers to maintain a high level of consumption during low wage apprenticeships.

These adverse incentive and adverse sorting effects of debt financed performance bonds, and the difficulty of firms knowing if workers are borrowing to pay performance bonds or using their own funds may explain why we rarely see firms selling jobs by demanding large performance bonds. Low wage apprenticeship programs are, on the other hand, far more common. Of course low wage apprenticeships are not necessarily a means of firms selling jobs.

A different criticism of the efficiency wage models is that they are dominated by piece-rate contracts or (if cheating by firms is a problem) by tournaments: wage payment schedules in which workers are ranked according to their performance and pay is a function of the worker's ranking. There are several problems with these tournaments.

First, if all firms were offering straight-time contracts a deviating firm offering a tournament may not be able to attract any employed workers. Suppose there is no upper bound on the distribution of types of workers. Each worker might think that only more able workers will

---

[7] Stiglitz and Weiss [1981] show why debt finance will induce borrowers to choose riskier actions.

join the firm offering the tournament, and hence would think that the expected wage for workers of his own type would be the wage associated with finishing last in the tournament. Even if workers didn't have these extremely pessimistic beliefs, uncertainty concerning which workers will apply to the tournament firm would deter applications from risk averse workers. Consequently, if only the unemployed apply to the tournament firm, and if the unemployed are likely to be low ability types, firms would not offer tournament wage schedules.

A second reason why firms would be reluctant to offer tournament wage schedules is that it is costly to measure the productivity of workers across different jobs. Even in very large firms there are rarely large numbers of workers doing the same job. Ranking workers across jobs, or even ranking salespersons who have different territories, can be very difficult. Workers may justly feel discriminated against—and the firm would be vulnerable to suits over race, sex or age discrimination.

Even in the absence of legal recourse, if workers view tournaments as inherently risky and susceptible to manipulation by managers favoring their friends, firms offering tournament wage schedules would need to offer higher expected wages in order to attract workers. This compensating wage differential coupled with the cost of ranking workers might make a tournament wage schedule less profitable than an appropriately chosen fixed wage.

Consequently, unemployment generated by efficiency wage considerations could persist even if firms had the option of offering quite complicated contrasts: including tournaments, low wage apprenticeships, or requiring workers to either buy their jobs or to post performance bonds.

1.2. Dismissal of workers

The final issue that shall be addressed in this monograph is why firms fire workers. Most of the work on adverse selection and incentive models of involuntary unemployment has been concerned with persistent job queues not with layoffs. In incentive models of unemployment such as Calvo [1979, 1985], Calvo and Wellisz [1978, 1979], Shapiro and Stiglitz [1984], Foster and Wan [1984], or Bulow and Summers [1986], it is typically assumed that firms fire workers whose performance is low rather than cutting their wages. (Note that this is an assumption, not a result of their analyses. In general these effort inducing models could be based on firms "punishing" poor performance by cutting the wages they pay workers, or giving those workers a less attractive new contingency wage contract, rather than firing them. Alternatively firms might fire some fraction of workers whose performance is low. Firms might also randomly monitor performance.) The assumption that firms fire workers whose output is low should be a result derived from the primitives of the model. That assumption is quite strong given the fixed costs imposed by turnover and the unnecessary turnover induced by monitoring errors.

We shall consider four explanations for why firms fire workers. Each of these explanations implicitly involves efficiency wage models that depart in some important respects from the standard ones mentioned above.

The first explanation appears in Stiglitz and Weiss [1983]. In that model workers have deterministic finite lives. In general, if the expected future work life of a worker declines with age, firms find it more profitable to employ young workers than older ones. Young workers have more future periods of work and hence the contingency contracts that can be written for them can more effectively influence their behavior. (Contract terms can be based on more contingency events and thus the importance of random events can be reduced.) Consequently in the Stiglitz and Weiss model, firms would like to fire all their experienced workers. However, the terms of the profit maximizing contracts only allow firms to fire workers whose output was low in the previous period (otherwise all workers would shirk). These contracts are enforceable since output is observable by a third party. Consequently a worker with high output who was fired could appeal the decision and force the firm to reinstate him. Because there is some random noise which causes a dispersion in the output of otherwise identical workers, those workers with particularly low output levels are fired.

The second explanation depends on introducing some residual informational asymmetries into the Guasch and Weiss [1982] model. In that model, an accurate pass-fail test is administered to workers. Those who fail receive a wage equal to their expected marginal product. Those who succeed are paid more than the value of their marginal product. The firm finances these high wages either by paying wages that are less than the value of workers' expected outputs while they are being tested or by charging application fees that exceed the true cost of administering the test. This combination of wages and application fees improves the firm's distribution of applicants. However, these contracts are not viable if other firms have some information about the productivity of the workers who failed the first firm's test. The other firms would hire those workers that they perceived to be the *best* of the first firm's failures. The workers that failed the test and were not hired by other firms would have a value to the first firm that is *less* than the wage they are being paid. (This is a consequence of the winner's curse). Consequently, a firm that is testing its workers would fire workers that failed its test rather than having other firms hire the best workers from among the workers that failed the test and were not fired.[8] Because the workers who pass the test are paid more than the value of their output the firm has less fear that those workers would be recruited by other firms.

A third explanation for why firms fire workers is based on a presumed correlation between attributes that are unobserved by the firm and the worker's best alternative opportunity. If the better types have better alternatives then the punishment associated with being fired is greatest for the lower ability types. Consequently firms may fire low performing workers as a means of improving their distribution of hired workers. These sorting motives will be accentuated if the ratio of the productivity to the reservation wage of the workers whose performance is low is not significantly lower than the ratio of the expected productivity to the reservation wage of a randomly selected applicant to the firm.

The final explanation for why firms fire workers is that the demoralizing effect of cutting wages or wage schedules could cause some workers to have very low output. That is, some workers may not respond rationally to the new contingency contract. Rather, they may engage in activities that are quite destructive to the firm. Since this explanation is based on non-rational behavior by workers, we shall not

---

[8] Of course, this argument depends on the first employer not being able to make a counter-offer. If the initial employer made the final offer then it is the raider that suffers the winner's curse and would not bid for workers. Greenwald [1986] presents a complete analysis of this case. In general some workers will not ask their firm to respond to outside offers, others will ask their firm to respond, while still others will conduct bidding wars between their current employer and the firm making the outside offer. Although these bidding wars are optimal (ex post) for the worker, they do not seem to occur frequently. This may be because firms will not make offers to workers whom they think will use those offers to elicit counter offers from other firms.

pursue it. However, it may be of significant practical importance. Even if the proportion of workers engaging in destructive behavior is vanishingly small, the damage that can be wrought may be so large as to make wage cuts of the form described by Radner [1981] and Dutta and Radner [1987] unprofitable to the firm.

1.3. Summary of results

Throughout this work, we shall draw attention to the welfare and policy implications of the models as they arise. We have tried, whenever possible, to give verbal and heuristic rather than mathematical and formal arguments.

Firms are not price takers in the analysis developed below. They act competitively in the sense that they choose contingency wage contracts and employment practices to maximize their profits.

Unless otherwise specified we use the term equilibrium to refer to a sequential Nash equilibrium as defined by Kreps and Wilson; and, unless otherwise specified, we assume that the order of moves is as follows: firms announce wage contracts; workers respond to these wage offers by applying to work for a firm or firms; firms then offer to hire some, or all, of their applicants; workers accept the most attractive offer they receive.

Most of the new results in this monograph are contained in Part I: the sections on the sorting effects of wages. We show that unobserved worker heterogeneity can lead to a serious misallocation of labor. Even in the simplest case where all workers are observationally identical, information asymmetries will result in too little output in the industrial sector, and may cause either under or over-employment in the industrial sector. We also construct an equilibrium for an economy in which there are several observationally indistinguishable groups: each group receives a different wage, and all but one group suffers unemployment.

Additional resource misallocation problems arise when there are several observationally distinct groups of workers. In Section 3 we show that there can be two observationally distinct groups of workers, one of whom is employed in the industrial sector and the other is unemployed, even though a randomly selected worker from the unemployed group has a comparative advantage in industrial employment relative to *every* employed worker. One of the more surprising results of Section 3 is an example in which worker heterogeneity is causing labor to be misallocated, but a mean preserving spread of the distribution of workers eliminates this efficiency loss. In Part II we are concerned with the effects of wages on worker behavior. The main new results there are to show that there may be a continuum of multiple wage equilibria when wages affect quit rates. Each of these equilibria corresponds to a different level of employment. We show that errors in the measurement of worker effort can *increase* the effort of workers: workers might contribute more effort than is called for in their contract. In our analyses of models in which high wages deter shirking we show that firms may choose not to monitor workers even if monitoring costs approach zero continuously as the level of monitoring goes to zero.

Part I. Worker Heterogeneity as a Cause of Unemployment and Layoffs

2. SINGLE WAGE EQUILIBRIUM

Adverse selection models of the labor market explain the failure of firms to cut wages in the face of an excess supply of labor by discussing how the composition of a firm's labor force would change in response to changes in the wage contract the firms offer. In these models, there is a heterogeneous labor force, and it is generally assumed that the reservation wages of workers are positively correlated with their labor endowments. Reservation wages are derived from the value the worker places on the activities he would pursue when unemployed. The possible activities include work in a non-industrial sector, such as household production or any form of piece-rate work in which problems of monitoring output do not arise.

Because reservation wages are positively correlated with labor endowments, if a firm were to cut the wage it offered, the workers that would be discouraged from applying to work for the firm would be the workers that the firm finds most desirable. Similarly, in these models, if a firm cuts the wage of its existing work force, the workers most likely to be induced to quit are the firm's best workers.

The reader may have noticed that we are phrasing our discussion in terms of firms announcing wages and each worker passively going to work for the firm offering him the highest wage. Suppose each worker were to announce a wage at which he were willing to work. Firms would infer that the worker's reservation wage is below the wage he announces: no worker offers to work for less than his reservation wage.

If there is an excess supply of labor at the market wage, an unemployed worker would not necessarily gain employment by offering to work at a lower wage. The act of offering to work at a lower wage would signal to firms that the worker is of relatively low quality, and may lower that worker's probability of being employed. Consequently, employers do not bid down the wages they offer workers, nor do they necessarily hire the worker who offers his labor at the lowest wage. The decrease in the average quality of their applicants from lowering their wage offer could outweigh their lower cost per worker. That is, the lower cost per worker could correspond to a higher cost per efficiency unit of labor.

In this section we shall present necessary and sufficient conditions for worker heterogeneity to lead to involuntary unemployment at a single wage. In later sections we construct multiple wage equilibria with involuntary unemployment at every wage, and show how worker heterogeneity leads firms to fire workers whose output is low rather than cutting their wage.

Before proceeding, it is appropriate at this point to define some of the terms we shall use and to explicitly present the assumptions we shall make. We assume that the production functions of all firms are the same. Their inputs into production are capital and labor where labor is defined in terms of labor inputs, not number of workers employed. The total labor input for a firm is the sum of the labor inputs provided by each of its workers. We let $q(w)$ denote the labor input of a worker with reservation wage w. The reservation wage of a worker is the lowest wage at which that worker would work for a firm in the industrial sector. We might consider the reservation wage as derived from the worker's value of leisure (larger if one has a rich spouse or large amounts of unearned income or significant unemployment benefits) or from the value of the worker's output in the non-industrial or household sector, whichever is greater. The non-industrial sector could be some form of self-employment such as agriculture in a less developed country, household work, or any job in which the worker's earnings are proportional to the worker's output.

2.1. Definition of unemployment

There is unemployment in an economy, if workers that are not employed in the high wage sector would be willing to work for a discretely lower wage than that being paid to workers who are observationally indistinguishable (or nearly indistinguishable) from them. Note that this is a stringent criterion. When appropriate we will use weaker definitions of unemployment. However, we do not define unemployment as a level of employment below that which would prevail in an economy with perfect information, nor are we defining all workers that are not employed in the industrial sector as being unemployed. In particular, there may be distinct groups of workers none of whom are employed, that we do not label as unemployed even if those workers have a comparative advantage in industrial employment. Of course, the exclusion of those types of workers from employment in the industrial sector does have important efficiency consequences, and we shall be concerned with those inefficiencies generated by informational asymmetries.

2.2. Other key assumptions

We assume that output in the non-industrial sector is a nondecreasing function of the total of the labor endowments of the unemployed. We normalize the price of the output of the non-industrial sector to 1, and assume the price of the output of the industrial sector is a decreasing function of the ratio of output in the industrial sector to output in the non-industrial sector. If that ratio is zero, the price of industrial output is assumed to be infinite so we always have some output in the industrial sector.

We shall assume $q'(w)$ is positive, so that workers with higher reservation wages are more productive.

We also let $Q(w)$ denote the expected labor input of a randomly selected worker with reservation wage less than w. (Throughout the following three sections we are assuming that effort is exogenous, so that the labor input of a worker is completely determined by his labor endowment.)

Letting $f(w)$ denote the density of workers with reservation wage w, we can write $Q(w)$ as

$$Q(w) = \frac{\int_0^w q(w)f(w)dw}{\int_0^w f(w)dw}$$

We assume the functions $q(w)$ and $f(w)$ are common knowledge, but that firms do not know the labor inputs of individual workers.

2.3. Characterization of equilibria

Now we can show that there can be an unemployment equilibrium with all firms offering the wages $w^* = \max\{\arg \inf(w/Q(w))\}$:$w^*$ is the highest wage that minimizes the firm's cost per unit of labor input, and

18   ANDREW WEISS

is commonly referred to as the efficiency wage. Consider the case where:

    a) the labor demand, if all firms were to offer wage w^*, is less than the labor supply of individuals with reservation wages less than or equal to w^*;
    b) the labor input of a firm employing L workers with average productivity $Q(w)$ is $LQ(w)$[1]
    c) there is no cost for workers to change jobs.

Then, the market equilibrium is characterized by all firms offering wage w^*.

We denote the production function of a firm by $g(\cdot)$, the price of non-labor inputs by r, and normalize the units of output in the industrial sector so that in equilibrium the price of output in the industrial sector is 1. Thus, from (b) the profit function $\pi(\cdot)$ of a firm utilizing K units of capital and hiring L workers at wage w is

$$\pi(w,L,K) = g(LQ(w),K) - wL - rK \qquad (2.1)$$

The approximation comes from $F(w)$ being a distribution and $g(\cdot)$ not being restricted to linear functions.

Let L^* be the number of workers that maximizes profits when the firm is paying wage w^*. We assume that for labor inputs greater than $L^*Q(w)$, the production function is concave in labor inputs.

To show that firms choose w^* to maximize (2.1), suppose, to the contrary, that there exists a wage $w_1 \neq w^*$, and labor force L_1 that maximizes profits when K units of capital are used. Let $L_0 = w_1L_1/w^*$, and let L^* be the labor force that maximizes firm profits when wage w^* is offered to all employees. Then,

$$\pi(w^*,L_0,K) = g\{L_0Q(w^*),K\} - w^*L_0 - rK$$
$$= g\{(w_1L_1/w^*)Q(w^*),K)\} - w_1L_1 - rK.$$

From the definition of w^*, $Q(w^*)/w^* > Q(w_1)/w_1$. Therefore

$$\pi(w^*,L_0,K) = g\{(w_1L_1/w^*)Q(w^*),K\} - w_1L_1 - rK >$$
$$g\{L_1Q(w_1),K\} - w_1L_1 - rK$$
$$= \pi(w_1,L_1,K).$$

---

[1] This is a strong assumption. Appendix A of Weiss [1988] presents an efficiency wage mode in which the relationship between labor input and the wage is due to the effect of wages on absenteeism. Under those circumstances assumption (b) will not hold.

From the definition of L^*, $\pi(w^*,L^*) > \pi(w^*,L_0,K)$. Therefore, w_1, L_1 would not have maximized firm profits.

Consequently, if the market equilibrium is characterized by job queues, so that at wage $\hat{w}$ the firm can hire as many workers as it wishes, the equilibrium wage minimizes the firm's cost per efficiency unit of labor. Changes in the firm's demand would affect the firm's choice of capital K and the number of workers it hires L, but unless the firm's labor supply constraint were to become binding, or the $Q(w)$ function were to change, fluctuations in aggregate demand would not affect the wage the firm offers.

Note that this result depends on several assumptions that we have made: the existence of a unique interior *supremum* w^* for $Q(w)/w$, the labor supply not being a binding constraint when w^* is offered by all firms, firm profits being non-negative when wage w^* is offered, and the firm's production function being specified in such a way that the labor endowments of each worker employed add together to give the total labor inputs of the firm.[2]

The intuition behind this result is that, just as with any other input to production, firms want to hire labor at the cheapest price per unit. The relevant unit, however, is not a worker. Since some workers are more productive than others, the relevant unit is an efficiency unit of labor. Suppose the average worker hired at $8.00 per hour is more than twice as productive as the average worker hired at $4.00. Then the $8.00 per hour workers are cheaper (in terms of cost per efficiency unit of labor) than the $4.00 per hour workers. Under those conditions, a firm would never hire workers at $4.00 per hour, regardless of the demand for its output or the price of other inputs. To simplify the exposition, unless specifically indicated otherwise, we shall assume that $Q(w)/w$ has a unique interior *supremum*. Of course the wage that maximizes $Q(w)/w$ is the "efficiency wage" w^*.

The determination of the efficiency wage, and its role in determining an equilibrium level of unemployment is illustrated in Figures 1 and 2. In Figure 1, we have drawn $Q(w)$ as a function of w. The wage w^* at

---

[2] Robert Solow (1979b) proved that the necessary and sufficient conditions for "a cost minimizing firm [to] leave its wage offer unchanged no matter how its output varies [is for] the wage [to enter] the production function in a labor augmenting way", i.e. as $g(Q(w)L)$, see Appendix A. Takaski Nageshi (1974) had previously showed that a production function of the form described was sufficient for wage inflexibility in the face of demand shocks.

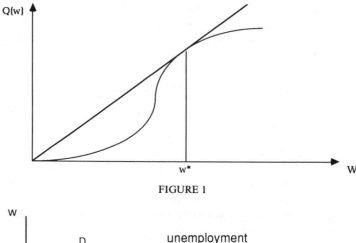

FIGURE 1

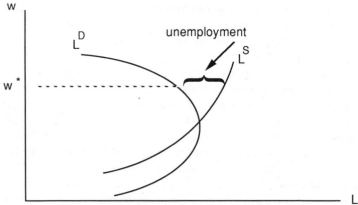

FIGURE 2

which a ray from the origin is tangent to this curve is the maximum of
$Q(w)/w$. We have referred to w^* as the efficiency wage. Recall that in a
perfect information model with no incentive effects of wage $w^* = 0$.

In Figure 2 we have plotted the labor demand and supply curves. We
continue to consider labor in terms of efficiency units, supplied and
demanded. Since labor, in efficiency units, is cheapest at the efficiency
wage, labor demand is greatest there. Aggregate labor demand in terms
of numbers of workers demanded would be greater at some lower wage
at which the number of workers embodied in an efficiency unit of labor
is greater. Consequently we have drawn the labor demand curve as
backward bending at w^*.

To avoid unnecessary complications, we have drawn an upward sloping labor supply curve. If labor supply at **w*** is greater than labor demand at **w*** there is an unemployment equilibrium. Equilibrium is defined as a choice by each firm of a wage, number of workers, and non-labor inputs such that, given the resulting output price, the labor input function **Q(w)**, and the labor supply and labor demand functions, no firm has an incentive to choose a different wage or quantity of labor or non-labor inputs. (To focus on the efficiency wage aspects of the problem, we assume throughout that firms act as price takers in the product market.) No firm would lower its wage since wage cuts would increase its cost per efficiency unit of labor: by construction, **w*** is the wage at which the cost of labor is lowest.

Indeed, *regardless of the position of the supply curve*, the equilibrium wage is never below **w***. This result is easily seen. If all firms were offering a wage below **w***, one firm could offer wage **w***. Since it is offering a higher wage than its competitors it would attract workers, and by paying the efficiency wage it would have lower labor costs and achieve greater profits than firms offering the lower wage. Note that in Figure 2 the impossibility of the equilibrium wage being below **w*** holds even if the labor supply and labor demand curves have a unique intersection, i.e. below **w***. Thus, although in that case there is a wage at which labor supply equals labor demand, no firm would offer that wage. A firm offering a higher wage, such as **w*** would of course attract workers, and would also lower its cost per efficiency unit of labor.

On the other hand, if the labor supply curve intersects the labor demand curve at a wage above **w***, the equilibrium wage can be above **w***. Firms compete for workers by offering the wage at which the labor supply and labor demand curves intersect. This is an equilibrium, since a firm offering a lower wage would fail to attract workers.

If a backward bending labor demand curve were to cause the labor supply and labor demand curves to intersect twice, the intersection at the higher wage is the unique equilibrium. This result can be seen in Figure 3.

If a wage less than **w*** were being offered by all firms, one firm could offer a slightly higher wage and make positive profits. A wage in the interval **[w*,w₁)**, cannot be an equilibrium since those wages are characterized by excess labor demand: firms would compete for workers by bidding up the wages they offer. Finally, for the usual reasons, the equilibrium can not be above **w₁**. Therefore **w₁** is the unique

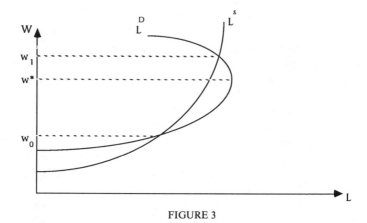

FIGURE 3

equilibrium given the labor supply and labor demand functions illustrated in Figure 3.[3]

Let us now return to the case where the labor supply curve is everywhere to the right of the labor demand curve. In that situation, as we argued, the market equilibrium is characterized by the efficiency wage being offered by all firms. Consider a change in the labor supply. Unless the labor supply falls sufficiently to cause the labor supply and demand curves to intersect, fluctuations in labor supply that hold constant $Q(w)$ will not affect the market wage. Consequently, the quantity of labor demanded will not be affected, and since we are considering excess supply equilibria, the quantity of employment will also remain fixed. On the other hand, fluctuations in the labor supply will affect the unemployment rate.

Conversely, fluctuations in labor demand that do not change the efficiency wage will not affect the market wage, but will affect both employment in the industrial sector as well as the unemployment rate. Notice that workers that are employed in the industrial sector are not necessarily those workers with a comparative advantage in industrial

---

[3] Note that our arguments bear no relationship to the market clearing analysis of markets in which the labor demand curve is downward sloping, and multiple intersections stem from a backwards bending labor supply curve. Note also that we are explicitly discussing uniqueness of equilibrium, not stability. This is because our definition of equilibrium is not market clearing but rather optimizing behavior by all participants.

employment: i.e. there may be two workers with reservation wages w_i and w_j respectively, where $q(w_i)/w_i > q(w_j)/w_j$ and type j is employed in the industrial sector and type i is not. Therefore, the market may be characterized by an inefficient allocation of labor. To see this, consider the case of job queues when the efficiency wage is being offered by all firms. Differentiating $Q(w)/w$ at $w = w^*$, and setting the derivative equal to zero we find

$$d/dw \left\{ \int_0^w q(v)f(v)dv/w \int_0^w f(v)dv \right\} = 0$$

or

$$w^* \int_0^{w^*} f(v)dv q(w^*)f(w^*) - \int_0^{w^*} q(v)f(v)dv \left[w^*f(w^*) + \int_0^{w^*} f(v)dv) \right] = 0$$

consequently

$$q(w^*) = Q(w^*) \left[1 + \int_0^w f(v)dv/w^*f(w^*) \right] \qquad (2.4)$$

Let

$$\tilde{q}(w) = q(w)/w;$$

and let

$$\tilde{Q}(w) = \frac{\int_0^w q(v)f(v)dv}{\int_0^w vf(v)dv}$$

so that $\tilde{q}(w)$ is the ratio of the labor input in the industrial sector of a worker with reservation wage w to that worker's reservation wage; and $\tilde{Q}(w)$ is the expected ratio of the labor input in the industrial sector of a randomly selected worker hired when wage w is offered to that worker's reservation wage. Substituting into (2.4), and rearranging terms we find,

$$\tilde{q}[w] = \tilde{Q}[w]\left\{\frac{\displaystyle\int_0^{w^*} vf[v]dv}{w^*\displaystyle\int_0^{w^*} f[v]dv} + \frac{\displaystyle\int_0^{w^*} vf[v]dv}{w^{*2}f[w^*]}\right\}$$

$$\frac{\tilde{q}(w^*)}{\tilde{Q}(w^*)} = \frac{r(w^*)}{w^*}\left[1 + \frac{F(w^*)}{w^*f(w^*)}\right] \tag{2.5}$$

Where r(w) is the expected reservation wage of a worker applying to a firm offering wage w, and F(w) is the cumulative distribution of workers with reservation wages below w.

The first term on the right hand side of (2.5) is less than 1 and the term in brackets is greater than 1. Depending on the relative magnitudes of the two terms, which of course depends on the distribution of reservation wages, the best worker hired has a comparative advantage or comparative disadvantage in industrial employment relative to the average worker hired.

If the right hand side of (2.5) were greater than 1, there would be workers with reservation wages above w^* that have a comparative advantage in industrial employment relative to the average worker being hired when the efficiency wage is offered. The allocation of labor would be improved—aggregate output increased—by raising the wage offers of firms and lowering the number of workers hired (holding the labor input of the industrial sector fixed).

Conversely, if the right hand side of (2.5) is less than 1, the best workers hired in the industrial sector would have a comparative disadvantage for industrial employment relative to the average worker hired. In that case, recalling that we have assumed that equilibrium is characterized by job queues, the allocation of workers to jobs could be improved by lowering the wage in the industrial sector and increasing the proportion of applicants hired so as to hold employment in efficiency units fixed. (Note that in the special case where $q(w) = aw$ where a is a constant greater than zero, the term in brackets is equal to 1 and the allocation of workers to jobs cannot be improved by changing the wage in the industrial sector.)

In either case, aggregate output would be increased by increasing employment (in efficiency units) in the industrial sector while holding wages fixed. Thus the conditions given in this model could be used to justify industrial policies that favor those sectors of the economy where informational asymmetries are most important.[4]

To show that there is too little employment, in efficiency units, in the industrial sector we differentiate representative firm's profit function with respect to the number of workers hired. Letting **w*** denote the wage offered by the representative firm, and letting **E** denote the quantity of labor inputs (efficiency units of labor) employed, we find

$$d\pi(w^*, L)/dL = (\partial g(.)/\partial E)Q(w^*) - w^* = 0. \qquad (2.6)$$

The firm hires workers until the point at which the marginal product of the average worker is equal to the wage **w*** it is paying. Because **w*** exceeds the average reservation wage of almost all of the firm's workers, at this point the reservation wage of the average employee, representing that employee's opportunity cost of employment in the industrial sector, is less than the value of that employee's output in the industrial sector. If each firm were to increase its labor inputs, holding the wage it offered fixed, aggregate output would increase.

This under-employment result is, of course, a standard result in the monopsonistic competition literature. But the reason for under-employment is different. In the monopsonistic competition literature the output of each firm is too low, because, by hiring an additional worker, the firm must increase the wage it pays all its intra-marginal workers. In the adverse selection model hiring an additional worker does not directly affect the wage of the other workers. However the cost to the firm of each worker hired is the reservation wage of the best worker hired. This cost is greater than the reservation wages of the intra-marginal workers hired. Consequently, in an unemployment equilibrium the opportunity cost to society of increasing employment in the high wage or industrial sector is less than the wage the firms pay.

When the labor supply constraint is binding so that there are no job queues, the usual result from the monopsonistic competition literature holds in this model. If individual firms face an upward sloping labor suppy curve, employment is too low because the only way a firm can

---

[4] As we shall see in Section 7, Bulow and Summers have argued that efficiency wage models, in which wages are chosen because of their effect on effort, support industrial policies that favor sectors of the economy in which the costs of monitoring worker effort is high.

increase employment is by increasing the wage of all workers. Under those conditions, attracting the marginal worker causes the wages of all the intra-marginal workers to increase.

In contrast to the standard monopsonistic competition models, in the adverse selection model the *number* of workers employed in the industrial sector is not necessarily below the level that would maximize total output in the economy. While there is always under-employment in *efficiency units* in the industrial sector, there may be over-employment in terms of *numbers* of employees. Over-employment in terms of numbers of workers employed in the industrial sector would arise if workers with low reservation wages and a comparative advantage in the non-industrial sector were working in the industrial sector. If the resource misallocation from these mismatched is sufficiently severe, then there could be too many workers employed in the industrial sector even though the amount of efficiency units of labor employed there is too low.

Over-employment in the industrial sector can only occur if the right hand side of equation (2.5) is greater than 1. Then the average worker in the industrial sector has a comparative advantage in the non-industrial sector relative to the marginal worker in the industrial sector. The allocation of labor between the industrial and non-industrial sectors could be improved by replacing low productivity (intra-marginal) workers in the industrial sector with high productivity workers whose reservation wages are above those of the marginal worker hired in the industrial sector. Since then fewer workers would be needed to maintain output in the industrial sector, a *fall* in employment in that sector and an *increase* in output in that sector could both follow from improvements in the allocation of labor between the industrial and non-industrial sectors. In particular, under these circumstances, a revenue-neutral government policy which combined a (small) tax per hour worked (or per employee) with a (small) wage subsidy would increase total output.

On the other hand, if the right hand side of (2.5) were less than 1, the allocation of labor would be improved by combining a per employee subsidy with a wage tax. Note that we are *not* allowing the social planner to have information that is not available to the firms, but only allowing the social planner to choose a wage and level of employment other than the profit maximizing ones.

Appendix A. Necessary and sufficient conditions for wage rigidity

Holding output **x** fixed, a firm chooses **L**, the number of workers, it hires and **w**, the wage it pays, to maximize **wL(x,w)**, where **L(x,w)** represents the number of workers the firm needs to hire to produce **x** units of output when it is paying the workers a wage of **w**. Thus **w** is chosen such that

$$L(x,w) + wL_w(x,w) = 0 \qquad (A.1)$$

For wages not to respond to changes in the demand for the firms output it is necessary that

$$L_x + wL_{wx} = 0. \qquad (A.2)$$

If at the values of **w** and **L** that solve the firm's maximization problem, there is an excess supply of labor, then (A.2) is also sufficient for changes in demand (that do not cause the labor supply constraint to be binding) to not affect the wage offer of the firm.

Since $\partial^2 \ln L / \partial x \partial w = (L \cdot L_{wx} - L_x L_w)/L^2$; given (A.1), (A.2) is equivalent to $\partial^2 \ln L / \partial x \partial w = 0$, or

$$\ln L = h(x) + j(w) + K, \qquad (A.3)$$

where **h(x)** is an arbitrary increasing function, **j(w)** is an arbitrary decreasing function and **K** is a constant. Rewriting (A.3) as

$$L = C\, a\,(x)/b(w),$$

where **a(·)** and **b(·)** are arbitrary increasing functions and **C** is a constant term, we find that when the labor supply constraint is not binding, a necessary and sufficient condition for wages to be rigid in the face of demand fluctuations is that output be determined solely by some function of the wage times the level of employment, or $x = a^{-1}(b(w)L/C)$. The reader may recall that in our earlier notation, the production function a^{-1} was referred to as **g(·)**, and $b(w)$ as **Q(w)**.

3. UNEMPLOYMENT WITH MULTIPLE WAGES

In Section 2 we analyzed single wage equilibria for a labor market in which there were heterogeneous workers, but all workers were observationally indistinguishable. In that section we assumed firms could not test workers and that it was costless for workers to change jobs. In this section we shall characterize multiple wage equilibria both for the labor market described in Section 2, and for labor markets with observable differences among workers and real costs of changing jobs.

3.1. Observationally indistinguishable workers

Figure 4 presents a $Q(w)/w$ function which can generate a two wage equilibrium with job queues at the high wage, for the model delineated in Section 2.

We have drawn Figure 4 such that the cost per efficiency unit of labor input is the same at w_0 and at w_1. Let us consider the case where, if all firms were offering wage w_0, there would be an excess demand for labor; while if all firms were offering wage w_1, there would be an excess supply of labor. We shall continue to assume that it is costless for workers to apply for jobs, so that rejected workers apply at other firms.

For this labor market there exists a two wage equilibrium with unemployment. The two wages offered by firms are w_0 and w_1. All workers with reservation wages below w_1 apply to work for the high wage firms, the firms offering wage w_1. Since by assumption there is an excess supply of labor at that wage, some of those applicants are not hired. Rejected applicants with reservation wages between w_0 and w_1 either work in the non-industrial sector or become unemployed. Rejected applicants with reservation wages below w_0 apply to work for the low wage firms. The number of high wage job offers is such that labor supply at the low wage firms equals labor demand.

Although there is an excess supply of labor at the high wage firms, if a high wage firm were to cut its wage offer, it would increase its labor costs. The low wage firms would decrease their labor costs if they could attract workers at lower wages. However, at the low wage there is not an

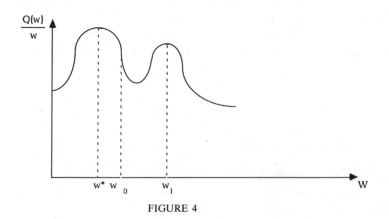

FIGURE 4

excess supply of labor. We term the rejected workers with reservation wages between w_0 and w_1 involuntarily unemployed, because they do not have jobs in the industrial sector and are worse off than identical workers (workers with the same reservation wages) that were hired by the high wage firms.

3.2. Groups of observationally distinct workers

We now consider the case of several groups of observationally distinct workers. The market equilibrium may be characterized by certain groups of workers suffering chronically high levels of unemployment, while other groups are fully employed.

We shall refer to workers that firms find observationally indistinguishable as belonging to the same cohort. In Figure 5 we illustrate the cost per efficiency unit of labor schedules for three cohorts of workers: a, b and c. As can be seen the efficiency wages of each cohort differs. In the market equilibrium firms may be competing for cohort b workers while no members of cohort a or cohort c are employed.

For example, at the efficiency wage w^*_b for cohort b workers, there may be an excess demand for labor. The wage paid cohort b workers would then be bid up, increasing the cost per efficiency unit of those workers. The market equilibrium would then be characterized by no unemployment, but only cohort b workers would be hired. For that

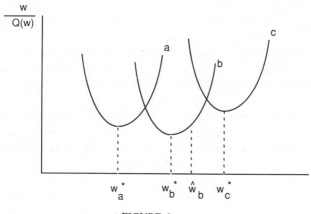

FIGURE 5

cohort of workers, labor demand equals labor supply. Despite the fact that employers are actively competing for type b workers no employer wishes to hire a type a or type c worker as long as the wage of the b workers generates a cost per efficiency unit of labor that is less than the minimum cost per efficiency unit of labor attainable from hiring from any other cohort, i.e. in Figure 5, if the excess supply of cohort b workers is exhausted at a wage less than $\hat{w}_b$, then neither type a nor type b workers are hired.

For a sufficiently large increase in demand, firms start hiring cohort a workers at their efficiency wage w_a^*. In that case we could have cohort b workers being hired at wage $\hat{w}_b$ with no job queues for cohort b workers, rationing of jobs for cohort a workers at wage w_a^* and no employment of cohort c workers in the industrial sector.

Note that we have said nothing about whether the workers hired from cohort b have a comparative advantage in industrial employment compared with the workers that would be hired from cohorts a and c at the respective efficiency wages w_a^* and w_c^*. That is, the intra-marginal type b workers may have reservation wages quite near to w_b^*, while the intra-marginal type a and type c workers may have very low reservation wages so that employing them at wages w_a^* and w_c^*, respectively, would have a major effect on their welfare; and if reservation wages reflect productivity in the non-industrial sector, employing types a and c rather than type b could increase total output.

The equilibrium employment of different cohorts of workers comes from their ordering according to their value of $\inf\{w/Q(w)\}$—the cohorts hired when labor demand is lowest are those for whom the minimum private cost per efficiency unit of labor is lowest. These are not necessarily the cohorts for which the minimum social cost per efficiency unit of labor is lowest, nor are they even the cohorts for which the social cost per efficiency unit of labor is lowest when firms pay each cohort the wage that minimizes their private cost per efficiency unit of labor.

Since within each cohort workers are observationally indistinguishable and all workers are paid the same wage, in general, employers would tend to favor relatively homogeneous cohorts of workers. When a cohort is homogeneous, fewer low productivity workers apply when the firm pays the reservation wage of the relatively more productive workers. This would imply that workers whose productivity is more readily observed by firms are more likely to be employed in the industrial sector.

We often find that workers whose backgrounds are familiar to employers (such as middle class white males) are more likely to be hired than workers with unfamiliar backgrounds. This may be because employers find it easier to accurately assess the expected productivity of members of familiar groups.[1]

It is apparent that the allocation of labor in markets with important informational asymmetries is not necessarily efficient—even in a second best sense. For example, it is possible for groups to be excluded from the industrial sector when a *randomly selected* member of the excluded group has a comparative advantage in industrial employment relative to *every* member of the cohort from which workers are being hired. In that case government policies that force firms to hire workers from the excluded group would improve the allocation of labor.

We can illustrate this result through a simple example. Consider two cohorts **i** and **j**. In cohort **i** all workers are identical. They have reservation wages of 1 and labor inputs of 2. In cohort **j** half the workers have reservation wages of 0.6 and labor inputs of 1; the other half have reservation wages of 3 and labor inputs of 10. A firm can hire workers from cohort **i** at an expected cost per unit of labor of 0.5. The firm's minimum expected cost per unit of labor when hiring from cohort **j** is 0.54545. This is achieved by hiring cohort **j** workers at a wage of 3; those workers have expected labor inputs of 5.5.

In equilibrium firms may only hire workers from cohort **i**, despite the fact that the expected *opportunity cost* per unit of labor input supplied when cohort **j** workers are hired at wage 3 is only 0.32727.[2] The opportunity cost per unit of labor of the employed cohort **i** workers is 0.5. Thus allocative efficiency would be increased if labor inputs were supplied from cohort **j** rather than **i**.

---

[1] Asymmetric information causes similar problems to arise in credit markets, and would explain why banks favor *employers* with characteristics with which they are familiar. Thus members of the excluded groups can not easily form their own firms. In this way our model explains why many of the most successful ethnic groups in a wide variety of countries are ones that developed formal or informal mechanisms to generate internal financing for investments by group members, why profit maximizing employers tend to favor workers from their own ethnic groups, and why members of groups that did not develop mechanisms to generate internal financing and did not fully assimilate into the main stream culture are disadvantaged both in access to investment funds and indirectly in access to the labor market.

[2] The computations are again straightforward: the expected opportunity cost of a type **j** worker hired at wage 3 is 1.8 and her expected labor input is 5.5. Dividing the former by the later yields 0.32727.

On the other hand, making a cohort of workers more heterogeneous, in the sense of a mean preserving spread (see Rothschild and Stiglitz [1970]), may *reduce* the equilibrium (and the minimum) cost per efficiency unit of labor for that cohort of workers. To illustrate this somewhat perverse effect, consider a cohort of workers with reservation wages uniformly distributed on the unit interval [1,2], and with a labor input function $q(w) = w$. If a finite number of workers are hired the cost per unit of labor in this economy will be strictly greater than 1: some market wage w will be paid and workers with labor endowments between 1 and w will be hired.

Assume that labor demand (in efficiency units) is $N/2$, where N is the number of workers in the cohort. Then firms offer the lowest wage at which aggregate labor demand is satisfied.

Now consider a mean preserving spread on the distribution of workers within this cohort. In the new distribution half the workers have a reservation wage, and corresponding labor input, of 1 and the other half have a reservation wage, and corresponding labor input, of 2. Since aggregate labor demand is $N/2$, in equilibrium firms pay a wage of 1 and have a cost per efficiency unit of 1. The mean preserving spread has decreased the cost of hiring workers from this cohort.

Note that the results derived thus far do not imply that as the number of observationally distinct groups of workers gets large, resource misallocations caused by asymmetric information disappear. That would only be the case if the groups are becoming more homogeneous, so that within each group all workers had the same (or very similar) labor endowments.

If the partitions are such that considerable heterogeneity remains within groups then, even if the groups are becoming more similar as the partition of the population gets finer, informational asymmetries will still have important welfare and resource allocation effects even as the number of observationally distinct groups are large. In particular, the expected utility of members of employed groups will be discretely higher than for members of unemployed groups, even if the two groups are very similar. Depending on how the population is partitioned, this fall in expected utility and the resource misallocation associated with informational asymmetries could even increase as the number of groups is increased.

To see this, consider an economy in which all workers were initially observationally indistinguishable. Now improve the availability of information so the labor force is partitioned into two observationally distinct groups: those with reservation wages above $\hat{w}$ and those with reservation wages below $\hat{w}$. Suppose, further, that the former group was very homogeneous and the latter group relatively heterogeneous. We could have full employment of the high reservation wage workers, at their efficiency wage and no industrial employment of the lower reservation wage workers, even if the latter had, on average, a comparative advantage in industrial employment. Since the unemployed workers are the workers with the low reservation wages, the difference in the expected utility of employed and unemployed workers would be greater after the partition then before the partition.

Consequently, improving the efficiency with which workers are identified does not necessarily improve social welfare. Workers gain from being identified as members of a homogeneous group, but they do not take into account the negative externality this identification may impose on other workers.

3.3. Costly job changes

Thus far we have only considered models in which job changes are costless. However, in adverse selection models, if there are costs to changing jobs the wage offers (or more generally the employment contracts) of firms affect the quality distribution of workers forthcoming at other wages. When a firm hires workers at wage w^* it improves the distribution of workers forthcoming for firms offering wages above w^*. Guasch and Weiss [1980a] refer to this phenomenon as "milking" the distribution—each firm only hires workers with reservation wages below the wage they are offering—hence the notion of taking the milk and leaving the cream. The distribution is thus enriched for firms offering a higher wage.[3]

When a worker can only apply to one firm, the market equilibrium

---

[3] Charles Wilson [1980a] analyzed these interactions among firms in a static adverse selection model of the used-car market. Guasch and Weiss [1980a] and Nalebuff and Stiglitz [1985] have analyzed these interactions in the context of dynamic models of the labor market. (Guasch and Weiss analyzed labor markets with a discrete number of firms; Nalebuff and Stiglitz analyzed labor markets with a continuum of firms). We shall first present a treatment of the static model, in which all firms simultaneously announce wage offers, before discussing the dynamic model, in which firms announce wage offers sequentially.

may be characterized by a continuum of wages being offered by different firms, and job queues at almost every wage offer. For each worker the choice of a firm to apply to is a function of his reservation wage, the distribution of wages offered by all firms, and the probability of being hired by each firm. Assuming workers are risk neutral with von Neumann-Morgenstern utility functions, a worker with reservation wage w_0 applies to the firm offering a wage w, with a probability of being hired p that maximizes $p(w - w_0)$, where p is determined in equilibrium from the choices of all other workers and the firm's (endogenously derived) demand for labor.

To see how the distribution of wages in the economy affects the distribution of workers forthcoming at any wage, consider two workers with reservation wages w_0 and w_1, respectively. Assume that workers will reservation wage w_0 are indifferent between applying to work for a firm offering a probability of being hired $\tilde{p}$ and a wage $\tilde{w}$, and firm offering the pair $(\hat{p},\hat{w})$. Without loss of generality, we can let $\tilde{w} > \hat{w}$; and therefore, $\tilde{p} < \hat{p}$.

For $w_1 > w_0$, workers with reservation w_1 will prefer the higher wage firm, the one offering wage $\tilde{w}$: this can readily be seen by differentiating $p(w)(w - w_1)$ with respect to w. The payoffs for success are the same for both workers, but the workers with higher reservation wages have higher payoffs, if they fail to be hired. Hence the worker with the higher reservation wage has a relative preference for contracts that have high failure rates—low values of p and correspondingly high values of w.

One implication of this analysis is that a firm offering a low wage would, by attracting workers with low alternative opportunities, be improving the pool of workers applying to a higher wage firm (assuming the probability of being hired at the higher wage is sufficiently low). Consequently there could be an equilibrium with several wages being offered, where the higher the wage the lower would be the probability of being hired.[4]

---

[4] Suppose wages are associated with separate geographic locations. Then, Robert Hall's empirical finding that cities which pay higher wages have higher unemployment rates provides some support for the model presented above. Weiss [1988] also finds a positive, and statistically significant, correlation between county unemployment rates and the wage a worker would expect to receive in that county.

3.4. A simple model of an equilibrium wage distribution

In this subsection we present a simple model to show that the results presented above continue to hold when there is an arbitrarily large, but finite, number of firms hiring workers.

We assume that firms are identical with constant returns to scale production functions up to some labor input E_0 which is a constraint on output so that $\partial g(\cdot)/\partial E = 0$ for $E > E_0$.[5] We assume E_0 is small relative to the aggregate number of efficiency units of labor available from each type of worker, but that the number of firms is sufficiently large that in equilibrium E_0 is not a binding constraint. We further assume that in equilibrium the price of the good produced in the industrial sector is a decreasing function of aggregate output in that sector.

Both firms and workers are risk neutral. We assume that if the expected payoff from applying to two different firms are the same for a worker, the worker applies to the firm at which his probability of being hired is greatest. Among firms offering the same contracts workers apply to each with equal probability.

Workers are observationally indistinguishable. There are n types of workers with reservation wages $r_1 < r_2 < \ldots < r_n$; and corresponding labor endowments $q_1 < q_2 < \ldots < q_n$. The sequence of actions is as follows:

First, each firm announces a wage offer and a number of job openings. The announcement of job openings is a commitment by the firm in the following sense. If, after the second stage in this sequence the firm has fewer applicants than the job openings it announced, it must hire all its applicants at the wage it announced. If the firm has more applicants than the number of job openings it announced, it must hire randomly from its pool of applicants until all the job openings it announced are filled.

Second, each worker observes all the wage offers and job openings announced by firms, and applies for work at one firm. We assume the search technology is such that workers cannot apply to more than one firm.

---

[5] This assumption is made to prevent a firm from offering wages slightly above the market wage for each type of worker, becoming a monopsonist in the labor market and consequently a monopolist in the goods market. Consideration of this rather far fetched scenario would tend to obscure some of the more important issues associated with efficiency wage models.

In equilibrium, the actions of firms and workers are optimal given the choices of all other firms and workers. We also need to specify what workers would do in response to an "out-of-equilibrium" wage offer(s) and number of jobs being offered. Workers have beliefs concerning how many other workers would apply to that firm(s). These beliefs, along with the wage being offered and the wages and probabilities of being hired by other firms, determine which workers (if any) would apply to the deviating firm(s). In equilibrium, beliefs are such that no firm would wish to change the contract it is offering. We assume beliefs are consistent with Bayes rule and are not contradicted by the equilibrium moves.[6]

In equilibrium, the number of applicants to firms offering wage w_i and the number of workers hired by those firms generate a probability of being hired for an applicant to those firms of p_i.

We order wage offers from the lowest to the highest. Thus p_1 is the probability of being hired when a worker applies to the lowest wage firm(s). If k wages are offered, p_k is the probability of an applicant to the highest wage firm(s) being hired. We continue to assume that workers with high reservation wages have high labor endowments—we refer to those workers as having high ability.

All workers with the same reservation wage are referred to as being the same type. A complete separating equilibrium is one in which each type of worker applies to work for a different wage. A complete sorting equilibrium has the following features:

a) Higher wage firms offer a lower probability of being hired.

b) Higher ability types work for firms offering higher wages, so that the existence of low wage firms lowers the cost per efficiency unit of labor for the high wage firms.

The negative relationship between wages and probability of being hired is obvious—no worker would apply to a firm if both the wage and the probability of being hired were greater at some other firm.

To show that higher ability types work for firms offering higher wages we recall our previous result that if one type of worker is indifferent between two wage-price pairs, types with higher reservation wages will prefer the wage-price pair with the higher wage. Thus the

---

[6] See Kreps and Wilson [1982] for a formal definition of consistent and rational beliefs.

greater is the reservation wage of a worker the steeper is his indifference curve in $\{w,p\}$ space. (Recall that high ability types have higher reservation wages.) The indifference curves of different types of workers only cross once. If we allow firms to have sufficiently pessimistic beliefs about the ability of workers applying to a firm offering an out-of-equilibrium wage, the single crossing property of the indifference curves, combined with the monotonic relationship between the slope of the indifference curves and the ability of the workers, is sufficient to ensure the existence of a separating equilibrium in which the higher ability types receive higher wages. We shall, however, present an example in which there is a separating equilibrium despite firms having fairly optimistic beliefs about which workers will respond to out-of-equilibrium wage offers.[7] (Once we show the existence of a separating equilibrium the characterization follows directly. No firm could be offering a high wage contract that attracted lower ability types than are being attracted by the low wage firms, because the high wage firm could offer the same wage as the low wage firm and increase its profits.)

Since low ability types are taking low wage jobs, it is apparent that if those jobs were no longer to be offered some lower ability types would apply to high wage firms, lowering the average productivity and raising the average cost per efficiency unit of labor at those firms. Thus low wage offers increase the profits of the high wage firms.

To further illustrate these points and to deal directly with the responses of workers to out-of-equilibrium wage offers, we construct an example of a multiple wage equilibrium with job queues at all but one wage. In this example the probability of employment, as well as the wage, serves as a sorting mechanism.

3.5. A multi-wage equilibrium with multiple job queues

We maintain all the assumptions expressed above: in particular, constant returns to scale technology up to a capacity limit, firms that are only informed about the distribution of workers in the economy but

---

[7] Beliefs play an important role in this analysis because workers do not know the probability of being hired by a firm offering an out-of-equilibrium wage. In other models in which the uninformed (firms) move first, such as Rothschild–Stiglitz [1976], there are problems with the existence of an equilibrium in pure strategies. These problems stem in part from the automatic responses of the informed participants in those models to out-of-equilibrium moves by the uninformed.

not about the identity of particular workers, risk neutral workers with von Neumann–Morgenstern utility functions.

The sequence of moves is that first firms make wage offers, then workers apply to firms. Finally, having observed the wage offers made by all other firms, each firm chooses a number of workers to hire.

The population consists of three types of workers: 5M type 1 workers, 2M type 2, and M type 3. M is a large positive constant. The reservation wages of type i, denoted r_i, is equal to i. The labor endowment of type i, denoted q_i, is equal to 2i.

We normalize output so that each efficiency unit of labor produces one unit of output, as long as the capacity constraint is not binding. We also assume that the price of output in the industrial sector is a decreasing function of the amount produced. The price is equal to 1 if production is $13\frac{2}{3}M$.

Finally we assume if the expected payoff from two different contracts is the same to a worker, the worker will apply for the contract at which he believes his probability of being hired is greatest.[8]

In the equilibrium we construct three wages are offered: 2, 4, and 6. The lowest wage firms hire all the lowest ability workers. The middle wage firms hire $\frac{1}{3}$ of the middle ability workers. The highest wage firms hire $\frac{1}{6}$ of the highest ability workers. Note that this model does not predict that the highest ability workers in the population are most likely to be unemployed, only that *among observationally identical* workers the highest ability workers apply for high wage jobs at which there are queues, and consequently are more likely to be self-employed or temporarily unemployed.

TABLE I

Number of workers	r_i	q_i	w_i	p_i
5M	1	2	2	1
2M	2	4	4	$\frac{1}{3}$
M	3	6	6	$\frac{1}{6}$

---

[8] This is simply a "tie-breaking rule" for cases in which workers are indifferent among two or more contracts. This rule may be interpreted as workers' having lexicographic preferences: firstly, concerning the expected payoff across contracts and, secondly, concerning the probability of being hired.

It is apparent from Table I that, in equilibrium, each firm has the same cost per unit of labor input. No firm can increase its profits by offering a wage that is being offered by another firm. Since the equilibrium is characterized by complete sorting, no firm can increase its profits by offering a pair of wages that improves the distribution of workers applying at its original wage (this possibility arises when there are partial separating, or pooling, equilibria.)

We still need to test for whether a firm can profitably offer a wage that is not being offered in equilibrium. In evaluating the profitability of these deviations we need to know the beliefs workers have concerning their probability of being hired by the deviating firm. While maintaining the assumption of common beliefs we shall allow those beliefs to be the most favorable ones from the viewpoint of the deviating firm. Since, as we shall show, no deviations are profitable given these extremely favorable beliefs, certainly no deviations would be profitable given more realistic beliefs.

The indifference curves of higher ability workers in $\{p,w\}$ space are steeper than the indifference curves of lower ability workers. (I_i denotes the indifference curve of a type i worker through the contract he is receiving in equilibrium.) Since the indifference curve of each type of worker (except the highest ability type) passes through the contract of the firm to which the next highest type is applying, a deviating firm can only attract type i and not type $j < i$ by offering a wage higher than the wage type i is receiving in equilibrium. This is illustrated in Figure 6.

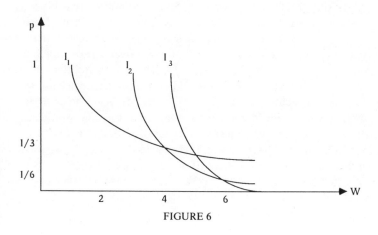

FIGURE 6

We can now show that the wages and employment levels described in Table I are an equilibrium, i.e. no firm could offer a different wage and make positive profits. A firm that wished to hire only type 2 workers would have to offer a $\{w,p\}$ pair satisfying $(w-2)p > \frac{2}{3}$, or $w > \frac{2}{3p} + 2$, where w is the wage offered by the deviating firm and p is the *belief* of workers concerning their probability of being hired by the deviating firm.

To dissuade the type 1 workers from applying, $(w-1)p < 1$ or $w < 1/p + 1$. Consequently, type 2 can only be attracted and type 1 deterred from applying, if $p < \frac{1}{3}$ and the wage is greater than 4. Clearly this wage offer would lose money.

Similarly a firm that wished to hire type 3 workers would have to offer a wage $w > \frac{1}{2p} + 3$, but to dissuade the type 2 from applying it would have to offer $w < \frac{2}{3p} + 2$. These inequalities are only satisfied for $p < \frac{1}{6}$ and a wage offer above 6, which loses money.

Let us now consider a deviating firm that attracts more than 1 type. If it wishes to attract types 1 and 2, it would have to pay a wage at least as great as $2\frac{2}{3}$, the lowest wage that can attract type 2 workers even if all workers were to believe their probability of being hired by the deviating firm were 1. Given the distribution of type 1 and 2 workers, if the deviating firm hired K workers its expected labor input would be $2\frac{4}{7}K$, while its wage bill would be $2\frac{2}{3}K$. Thus the deviating firm would find that its cost per unit of labor input was higher than the cost for firms offering the equilibrium contracts.

If a firm wished to hire only types 2 and 3, the lowest cost at which it could do this would be at a wage of 5. This would be feasible only if workers believed the probability of being hired by a firm offering a wage of 5 was $\frac{1}{4}$, corresponding to the point where the indifference curves of type 1 and 3 intersect in Figure 6. Given the proportions of type 2 and 3 workers in the population, if the deviating firm hired K workers its expected labor input would be $4\frac{2}{3}K$, and its wage bill would be 5K. Thus it would be made strictly worse off from the deviation.

Finally, we can consider a firm offering a contract that would attract all three types of workers. The minimal cost for this contract would be a wage of $3\frac{1}{2}$, which is the minimum wage needed to attract type 3 workers given the most optimistic beliefs. If K workers were hired by this firm, its expected labor input would be 3K while its wage bill would be $3\frac{1}{2}K$. Thus the deviation would increase the firm's cost per unit of labor input.

As this example shows, there can be multiple wage equilibria with unemployment at every wage except the lowest one.

3.6. Generalizations

The example is sufficiently flexible to encompass models with any (countable) number of types. In the example the unemployed type 3 workers do not have a comparative advantage in either the industrial or non-industrial sector. However, it is clear that for sufficiently small decreases in r_3, the nature of the equilibrium is not change: the type three workers remain the least likely to be employed in the industrial sector, even though they would now have a comparative advantage in industrial employment. Thus, as we saw in Section 2, with informational asymmetries, the market equilibrium may be inefficient in two respects: both the quantity of labor and distribution of types of workers allocated to the industrial sector may be suboptimal.

Note that throughout this analysis we assumed firms do not hire the rejected applicants of the high wage firms. In equilibrium those workers have identified themselves through their application decision so one might think that another firm could profitably offer them a wage that is above their reservation wage but below the value of their labor input. This argument is incorrect. Remember firms make their wage offers before workers apply for jobs. Suppose a firm made the following wage offer: we shall pay a wage of 5 to workers that were rejected by a firm offering a wage of 6. By making this offer the second firm is effectively raising the probability of a worker applying to a high wage firm being hired and lowering the expected wage conditional on being hired. As we see in Figure 6 any lower w–higher p combination that attracts type 3 will also attract type 2 so both the high wage firm and "scavenger" firm would be hiring types 2 and 3 (and possibly type 1 as well). However, a firm paying wage = 6 and hiring any type 1 or 2 workers will lose money. Once the high wage firm becomes aware of the contract being offered by the scavenger firm, it would not hire any workers. Workers would also know this, and consequently workers would only be attracted to the high wage firm by the wage offers and hiring probabilities of the scavenger firm. The scavenger firm that wished to attract any type 3 workers would have to offer a contract along their indifference curve. But, as we've seen, the only contract on that indifference curve that does not lose money is the one offered in the original equilibrium.

4. LAYOFFS AND FIRING OF WORKERS: AN ADVERSE SELECTION EXPLANATION

Thus far, we have focused on how unobserved worker heterogeneity can explain persistent job queues—involuntarily long term unemployment—and can cause a misallocation of workers between the industrial sector and the non-industrial sector or unemployment. In this section we shall show how unobserved worker heterogeneity can also explain why firms fire workers.

If all workers were identical, or if all firms were perfectly informed about the productivity of workers, and both firms and workers were risk neutral, a firm would respond to a fall in the value of a worker's output by cutting the worker's wage. If the value of the worker's marginal product were greater elsewhere (or if his utility from unemployment exceeded the wage), the worker would quit.

However, if a firm is imperfectly informed about the productivity of its workers, the firm would care about which workers would be induced to quit by a wage cut. The firm would be concerned that the workers that quit could be the ones the firm most wants to retain—workers whose productivity exceeds their wage.

The adverse selection effect of quits is due to attributes that affect the worker's productivity, and are not observed by the firm, but are observed by either the worker or other firms. Consequently, the wage at which a worker will quit will, in general, be positively correlated with aspects of the worker's performance.

The effect of adverse selection considerations on turnover occurs even in the simplest models presented in Sections 2 and 3. If a firm paying the efficiency wage w^* encounters a fall in demand (that does not affect reservation wages), it would fire workers rather than cut wages.

If we consider the situation with several cohorts of workers described by Figure 5 of Section 3, we would find that a firm would respond to a fall in demand by laying off workers in cohorts that are being rationed before it cuts the wages of workers in non-rationed cohorts. If the model were reformulated in an inter-temporal context we would find that the last workers hired would be the first fired.

To see this, suppose a firm is hiring from several different cohorts of workers, and that there are job queues at the wage offered cohort c workers in Figure 5: those workers are being paid their efficiency wage w^*_c. The firm's cost per efficiency unit of labor would rise if it cut the wage of workers who are receiving their efficiency wage. Workers from other cohorts, a or b, would not suffer wage cuts because the first order conditions for profit maximization imply that only the marginal unit of labor hired in cohorts a or b have a cost to the firm per efficiency unit of labor as great as the cost of a randomly selected worker from cohort c when the latter are paid w_c^*. Thus, any wage cut that induced a finite number of quits from cohorts a or b would induce workers to quit whose total cost to the firm per efficiency unit of labor is smaller than the cost of workers of cohort c that are being randomly fired. Workers of cohorts a or b would not suffer wage cuts until all members of cohort c were fired. Once all the cohort c workers were fired further falls in demand would cause wage cuts, rather than layoffs, until cohort a workers were receiving their efficiency wage w^*_a, and type b workers were being paid $\hat{w}_b$. At that point, any further falls in demand would cause layoffs of type a workers.

If the initial equilibrium were not characterized by job queues, so that no cohort of workers were receiving its efficiency wage, then a fall in demand would first precipitate wage cuts for all the workers hired until one cohort was receiving its efficiency wage. At that point further falls in demand would induce layoffs rather than wage cuts.

The arguments presented above to explain layoffs are similar to those we have already presented to explain the persistence of job queues. The source of the informational asymmetries remains information about a worker's productivity that is known to the worker but not to the firm. The layoffs and firing that can be explained using the models presented in Sections 2 and 3, are due to falls in demand. If the fall in demand affected the whole industrial sector, the laid off workers would either become unemployed or would become employed in the non-industrial sector. If the fall in demand did not affect the entire industrial sector, some of the laid off workers would obtain jobs with other firms in the industrial sector.

However, workers are also fired for low performance even when demand is high. It is not uncommon for firms to be firing some workers while hiring others to fill the vacant positions. One explanation for this practice is based on asymmetric information across firms. Outside firms have information about the productivity of some of a firm's workers that is not known to the firm. Consequently, if a firm were to cut the wages of workers whose observed output were low, the best of those low performance workers would be the most likely to quit.

When employers observe that "if they cut wages their best workers would quit", they are arguing that other firms would induce their best workers to change jobs (even during the depression of the 1930s there was considerable hiring of workers—estimates of hiring rates during that period range as high as 2% per month). Firms seem to be aware of information other firms have about the productivity of their workers that is either not available to the first firm, or that the first firm can not use. This argument does not imply that the outside firms have more or better information than does a worker's own employer; only that the raider has information (or a strategy) that is not available to the firm, and that consequently enables the raider to recruit selectively. For example, customers may know of certain personality traits of repair persons or salesmen of their suppliers. Conversely, suppliers of technical equipment may be aware of certain dimensions of the technical expertise of employees of their customer of which the employees' managers are not aware. In academia or research firms employees of competitors may be better able to evaluate the expertise of a given worker in their own specialty than can the worker's employer. (This is one reason why universities ask for outside letters when making tenure decisions.)

For the remainder of this section, we shall assume that outside firms observe some attributes of workers that are not observed by their employers.

4.1. A model of dismissals

We shall describe the labor input contributed by a worker as being determined by a set of attributes **A**. A proper subset of these attributes, denoted by **G**, are costlessly observed by all firms and workers. We label workers with the same observed **G** attributes as being members of the same cohort. There are also attributes of a worker that only the worker himself can costlessly observe. These attributes are denoted by **W**. Workers with the same **G** and **W** attributes are labeled as being the same group. Within a group workers have different productivities. There are also attributes **Z** that affect productivity, but are not observable by either workers or firms. That is, elements of **Z** are not elements of **G** or **W**.

Productivities within a group are distributed according to a symmetric increasing hazard rate distribution (such as the normal or uniform).[1] The distributions across groups is such that $f_i(q) = f_j(q - \Delta)$ for $i \neq j$, where $f_i(q)$ is the normalized density of workers with productivity q belonging to group i. Thus, for any two groups belonging to the same cohort, the normalized distribution of productivities for one of the groups can be obtained by adding a constant term to the productivity of members of the other groups. That is, the distributions differ only in their means, the higher moments of the distributions are the same. An example of the productivity distribution for two groups within the same cohort is presented in Figure 7.

We assume that for every firm there are some workers with attributes that affect their productivity, and that are not observed by the employer, but are observed by at least one other firm.

Firms can administer an accurate, albeit imprecise, pass–fail test of the productivity of each of their workers. (In practice, the test often takes the form of a low wage probationary period or apprenticeship program for newly hired workers). Both the worker and the firm can observe whether the worker has passed the test, and this test result can be verified by an outside observer. Thus, if a worker passes the test and the initial contract promised the worker a particular wage conditional on passing the test, the worker can force the firm to honor its commitment.

Firms can choose the difficulty of the test: the minimum productivity required to pass the test. We assume that the distribution of available tests, and the distribution of workers is such that, within every group of workers, there are some workers whose productivity is so low that they would fail every test and others whose productivity is so high that they

---

[1] An increasing hazard rate distribution is one where $\dfrac{d}{dq}\left(\dfrac{f(q)}{1 - F(q)}\right) > 0$. These assumptions imply that if the mean productivity in group i is higher than in group j, then members of group i will also have a higher expected productivity conditional on their productivity being above or below some arbitrary level. These assumptions ensure that holding wages fixed a firm would prefer to hire members of group i rather than j conditional on either workers passing, or failing, an accurate but imprecise test of their productivity. This, and other properties, of increasing hazard rate distributions are proven in Bryson and Siddiqui (1969).

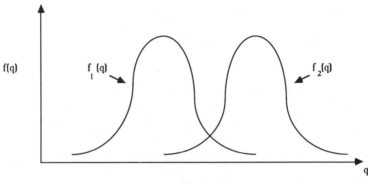

FIGURE 7

would pass every test. (This assumption is needed for the expected productivity of a randomly selected worker with a particular employment record to be well defined for every wage-test combination.)

Firms can charge workers a fee to be tested. When the test takes the form of a probationary period or entry level job, the fee can be viewed as the difference between a worker's wage during that period and the value of his output during that period. If this fee exceeds the testing cost of the firm, then, in equilibrium, a worker's expected wage after the testing period is completed exceeds his expected productivity. Contracts specify whether firms can fire workers who failed (or passed) the test, as well as wages conditional on whether the worker passed the test. Any firm can costlessly learn the wage of any worker.

Finally we assume that firms do not respond to outside offers. This last assumption reflects the usual policy of firms as reported in the *Wall Street Journal* (July 6, 1986).[2]

---

[2] There are several reasons why firms do not respond to outside offers. First, employees who don't intend to leave would be encouraged to redirect their activities in ways that would elicit high outside offers. This redirection would cause a misallocation of effort. The misallocation is not just in time spent on job search, but also in pursuing activities whose results are visible to outside firms in preference to activities whose results are only known to one's employer. Second, employers usually cannot verify the outside wage offers made to their workers until they are accepted, hence by responding to outside offers firms would provide an incentive to their workers to invent nonexistent outside offers. Finally, matching outside offers would cause morale problems both among workers who did not receive those offers and who are as productive but lower paid than the workers who did receive outside offers, and among the recipients who might resent the fact that their pay increase was delayed until they received the outside offer. This last point was stressed by the *Wall Street Journal*.

Thus the contracts offered to newly hired workers by firms that test their workers specify a fee that their applicants must pay to be tested (a wage to offer newly hired workers), a wage conditional on whether the worker passes or fails the test, a probability of continued employment for workers who pass (fail) the test, and a productivity level q that workers must satisfy in order to pass the test. The contracts offered by firms that do not test workers simply specify a wage paid to workers. Firms choose their level of employment, assuming the contracts they offer attract a sufficient number of applicants. Note that we are assuming that firms offer a constant wage. If workers differed according to their quit propensities firms might also wish to offer steeply sloped wage-tenure profiles as a means of attracting workers with low quit propensities.[3]

As was suggested in footnote 1 of this section, from our assumptions about the distribution of productivities within and across groups of workers, the expected productivity of a worker who passes the test is an increasing function of his probability of passing the test. Consider two workers belonging to two groups within the same cohort. If both pass the same test the worker belonging to the group with the distribution farthest to the right in Figure 7 has the highest expected productivity.

Therefore, a firm could increase its profits if it could deter applications from members of group 1 in Figure 7. That is, firms would try to have workers self-select themselves according to the information which the workers possess about their own attributes W and would elicit applications only from workers whose productivity, conditional on the information known to the firm, is high. Firms that test workers can do this by increasing the reward to workers who pass the test and penalizing workers who fail the test. These contingency wage offers would encourage applications from workers who believe their probability of passing the test is high (these are also the workers whose expected productivities conditional on their test scores are high). They would discourage applications from workers who believe that they are less likely to pass the test. However, a firm cannot pay workers a wage lower than the expected productivity of their applicants who fail their test. If they did, other firms would bid away those workers.[4]

---

[3] See Salop and Salop (1976).

[4] Because we do not allow firms to respond to outside offers, outside firms do not confront a winner's curse that would cause them to lower the value of their offers, or to refrain from making any offers to the employees of other firms. Greenwald [1986] has

Consequently, the only scope for rewards and punishments open to the firm is to pay workers who pass the test a wage greater than their expected productivity, and to recoup these losses, as well as the firm's testing costs, by charging workers a fee to be tested. The firm makes positive profits on its young workers and loses money on its older workers.

If at least one outside firm has information about a firm's employees that is not known by the firm, the firm would have an incentive to fire the workers that fail its test.

The reason that workers who fail the test would be fired is that whenever other firms have private information about worker productivity, a firm paying workers a wage equal to the firm's *estimate* of the worker's productivities would find that the workers most likely to quit are the workers whose wage was low relative to their labor inputs. The firm would be left only with those workers whom it finds, in retrospect, it does not want. The importance of this winner's curse depends largely on the importance of firm-specific human capital relative to residual private information by workers and other firms, and on whether the firm responds to outside offers. (We are implicitly assuming that the wage paid to workers that pass the test is sufficiently high, relative to the private information available to outside firms and the degree of worker heterogeneity, that outside firms would not make offers to any of those workers. Alternatively we could have assumed that in choosing their contingency wage schedules, firms take into account the (future) outside offers that will be made in response to these wage schedules.)

This problem of the winner's curse is most severe in the case of relatively young workers who fail the firm's test. Here the relevant alternative to working for the present employer is not retirement, but rather working for another firm. The first (testing) firm wishes to penalize failures as a means of discouraging low ability groups from applying to work for the firm. However, even in a separating equilibrium the firm cannot pay the workers a wage that is less than or equal to their expected productivity. As we've pointed out, this is because other firms have information about some of these workers that is not available to their employer. If this group of heterogeneous workers

---

(^{4} cont'd) analyzed equilibrium wage patterns when firms respond to outside offers and the outside firm is not permitted a counter-response. He has shown that under those conditions, unless there is some exogenous turnover, no outside offers are made.

were all paid a wage equal to the average productivity in the cohort, another firm could use its private information to hire workers whose expected productivity conditional on this private information, as well as the public information revealed by the decision to work for the firm in question and their score on the firm's test as revealed by their post-test wage, exceeds the worker's present wage.[5]

For any wage paid failures, the testing firm would face a residual adverse selection problem—the best workers among these low productivity failures would quit. Unless the firm is paying a wage less than or equal to the lowest possible productivity of any worker in its pool of applicants, the firm would always find that it is paying the failures that it retains more than their expected productivity. Consequently, firms will either pay workers who fail their test a wage that induces (almost) all their workers to quit, or will fire workers that fail their test. If the lowest productivity level in a firm's applicant pool is below the legal minimum wage then the firm would fire all the workers that failed its test.

Hence, if a separating equilibrium exists, it will be characterized by low wage apprenticeships culminating in a test. The workers that pass the test are paid more than the value of their labor input. In general, the workers who fail the test are fired.[6]

Note that this argument rests, not on other firms being better informed than the worker's employer, but only on one other firm having some information that is not available to the employer.

To summarize the argument offered above: from the contract the employer offers, other firms can infer the group(s) of workers attracted

---

[5] While we have precluded firms from selectively matching outside offers as in Greenwald (1986), this restriction could be justified within the context of the model presented above by assuming that the only private information of the firm is whether the worker passed the firm's test. Then the post-apprenticeship wage a firm pays would reveal all its private information. If a firm tried to conceal this private information by paying workers who failed its test the same wage as it paid workers who passed, the firm would not be able to avail itself of the self selection effects of contingency wage contracts.

[6] A proof of this result appears as Proposition 3 in Guasch–Weiss [1982], for the case where workers pay a fee to be tested and no firms have private information concerning the productivity of the employees of other firms. It is trivial to modify the proof for the case whether other firms have private information so that failures are fired—in the Guasch–Weiss paper, employers are indifferent between firing failures and cutting their wages. Similarly, the application fee in the proof can be interpreted as a low wage apprenticeship program.

to that firm. From the wage the worker is receiving, other firms can infer whether the worker passed or failed the firm's test. Hence, by using their private information firms can profitably hire from any pool of workers that are being paid a wage equal to their expected productivity.[7]

4.2. Mandatory retirement as a form of layoff

Edward Lazear (1979) has pointed out that wage-seniority patterns in which the young workers are paid less than the value of their labor input, while the older workers are paid more, can explain mandatory retirement—which is of course a form of firing.

To achieve an efficient allocation of labor, and thus to maximize the expected lifetime utility of workers, workers should retire when their value of leisure exceeds their productivity for the firm. But when older workers are paid a wage in excess of the value of their output, workers will not voluntarily retire at the correct time. They will voluntarily retire only when their value of retirement leisure exceeds the difference between their income as a worker and their income as a retiree. Because workers will not, in general, choose the optimal time to retire, mandatory retirement improves the allocation of labor between work and leisure.

One could argue that the same effect would be achieved by lowering the wage of workers that the firm estimates contribute labor inputs that are less valuable than their value of leisure; thus inducing those workers to quit. In Lazear's model quit inducing wage cuts would have the same effect as a mandatory retirement rule. However, if a firm were to use wage cuts to induce its older workers to quit, it could face severe adverse selection problems.

If all workers were induced to quit by the wage cut, then, of course, the wage cut is equivalent to firing workers. If, however, not all workers were to quit, the firm would have to be concerned whether the expected productivity of a worker *conditional on not quitting* is less than the wage the firm is offering.

There are many reasons why wage cuts may induce the "wrong" workers to quit. For example, workers who have "retired on the job", and whose-on-the-job retirement is unobserved by the firm, are

---

[7] This same argument shall be used in Section 7 to explain why firms fire workers that are caught shirking rather than punishing shirking by cutting the wages of those workers.

unlikely to be induced to quit by a wage cut. Similarly, workers who are stealing from the firm are unlikely to be induced to quit. On the other hand, those experienced workers who are paid less than the value of their output will be more likely to quit, if some aspects of their productivity that are not observed by the firm are observed by other firms or can improve the workers earnings if self-employed. (Anecdotal evidence suggests that when firms offer retirement incentive plans they find that the workers they most want to retain are those that avail themselves of the retirement option.)

4.3. An extension to multiple tests

One obvious extension of the model presented thus far would be to allow firms to offer a sequence of tests. This sequence would correspond to the process of periodic re-evaluations a worker undergoes as part of his normal career progression. Developing a full model with sequential tests would be beyond the scope of this monograph. However, we conjecture that a model of that sort could help explain why turnover declines with seniority.

There are two reasons why we would expect sequential testing to cause turnover to decline with seniority. The first explanation relies on the sorting effect of tests; the second on job matching.

Consider a firm first offering a sequence of pass–fail tests. By charging an application fee (possibly in the form of low wages during the trial periods) and firing workers that fail the first test, a firm will deter applications from low productivity workers. The workers that pass a given sequence of tests may all have had the same beliefs about their productivities prior to applying—in the language used previously they are members of the same group. Thus, firing workers who pass all the tests in that sequence, but fail some subsequent test(s), imposes risk on the workers without improving the mix of applicants. Indeed, for almost all tests there is a trade-off between the sorting effects of penalizing failures and the additional risk which tests force workers to bear if workers are imperfectly informed about their true productivity, or if the tests are inaccurate. We would expect the tests that are most likely to result in workers being fired to be administered early in a worker's tenure. This would increase the impact from the sorting effects of those tests, and decrease the expenditures on investments in firm specific human capital for workers whose expected future tenure is low.

The second, and perhaps more compelling, reason why sequential tests would cause turnover to decline with seniority is one that hinges on job matching. Many of the tests a firm administers will determine various attributes of the worker, and will improve the match between the worker and the jobs available in the firm. We might even think of various job assignments as tests that inform the firm about the co-workers with whom a particular employee is most productive. That information will greatly increase the value of the worker to the firm but is of much less value to other firms. Similarly, a test that optimally assigns workers to jobs at a particular firm, results in fully-revealing job assignments only if another firm offers the same set of jobs. Hence test results may be viewed as a form of firm specific human capital that would discourage turnover.

As workers get older, the initial test results may lose their validity. If the worker is likely to retire soon, firms may not wish to invest in new tests. Hence turnover may stop declining after a certain age and may even increase. This pattern for job matching corresponds to depreciation of firm specific human capital in the traditional human capital models.

4.4. Non-existence of equilibrium

Thus far we have explained why a separating equilibrium can be characterized by firms firing low performance workers. We have not shown that separating equilibria exists. Indeed, in general, pure-strategy separating equilibria do not exist.[8]

There are two reasons why there may not be a separating equilibrium in this model. First, if the cost of testing is too high, no firm would wish to test workers. Hence all workers of a given cohort, with reservation wages below the wage offered by the firm, would be pooled together. In this case an equilibrium would exist, but it would not be a separating equilibrium.

The second, more fundamental, reason for nonexistence is that a firm which tests its workers can only attract workers of a single group. This is because the indifference curves of different groups of workers have different slopes in {wage-pass, wage-fail} space. A firm offering a

---

[8] We are only concerned with pure-strategy equilibria. The mixed strategy equilibria constructed by Rosenthal and Weiss [1984] suggest that when pure-strategy equilibria do not exist in models of this sort the mixed strategy equilibria are not very reasonable.

single contract and attracting more than one group of workers would find that a competing firm could offer a contract that attracts only the best groups that the firm is hiring, i.e. the workers that the firm is making the greatest profit on.

Thus if a separating equilibrium exists, each firm must be attracting only one group of workers. However, it must be necessary then for a firm attracting workers that are members of neither the highest nor the lowest ability groups to offer contingency wage contracts that deter both the higher and lower ability workers from applying. Of course, the set of contracts offered by each firm must generate non-negative profits. (Stiglitz and Weiss [1989] show that if no two types of workers can be indifferent between the same two contracts, and some minor technical conditions are satisfied, each contract generates zero profits.)

The basic condition for a separating equilibrium to exist is that there must be a set of tests offered such that the higher expected pay from the contract designed for the high ability group be sufficient to attract high ability workers despite their higher probability of passing the test offered to the low ability workers. (Recall that for the test designed for the lower ability workers to deter applications from even lower ability workers, the wage for a worker that passes the low ability test must exceed the value of that worker's expected productivity.) For contracts to satisfy this condition, firms must choose tests such that differences in expected productivities relative to differences in the probabilities of passing the test are greater for high ability groups than for low ability groups. Intuitively, if the probability of passing were to increase too rapidly compared with the increase in expected productivity, members of the higher ability groups would take the test: the expected reward (overpayment) due to their high probability of passing the test would outweigh their lower expected (unconditional) wage from being pooled with a lower ability group.

Formally, if we let n denote the highest ability group that is not tested, Q_i the expected productivity of group i workers, and p_j^i the probability of group i workers passing the test offered by firm j, then:

A separating equilibrium exists if, and only if, there exists a set of tests inducing probabilities of passing the test p_j^i such that $\forall$ $a,b \geqq 0$ and $i - b \geqq n$

$$(Q_{i+a} - Q_i)/(p_{i+a}^i - p_i^i) \geqq (Q_i - Q_{i-b})/(p_i^i - p_{i-b}^i). \qquad (4.1)$$

Proof: See Guasch and Weiss (1982).

In Guasch and Weiss [1982] monotonicity properties on $F_i(q)$ are presented that ensure that (4.1) holds. Those properties can be interpreted as follows: if the difference in the expected productivity of a random related member of the highest and lowest groups being tested is smaller than the range of productivities (within a group) over which $f_i(q)$ is increasing, the conditions for a separating equilibrium among the tested groups will be satisfied.

Figure 8 illustrates conditions under which a separating equilibrium cannot exist, even if the cost of testing workers is zero. The diagram describes the case in which there is only one pass–fail test available to firms. S_i denotes the expected productivity of group i workers that pass the test. π_i denotes the locus of zero profit contracts for a firm hiring only group i workers. Because we have assumed workers are risk neutral and uninformed about their true productivity, the slope of π_i is the same as the slope of the indifference curves of members of group i. This slope is $1/p_i$.

The reason a separating equilibrium fails to exist in Figure 8, is *not* because it can be broken by a pooling contract—the reason for non-existence of a separating equilibrium in Rothschild and Stiglitz [1976]. Rather, non-existence arises because there are no contracts on the zero profit line of the type 2 workers that dissuade applications from both type 1 and type 3 workers, when those workers are being offered contracts on their respective zero-profit lines. Consequently, there does not exist a set of zero profit contracts that separates the workers.

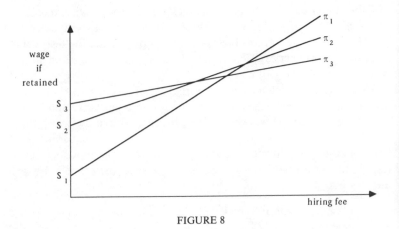

FIGURE 8

Part II. Incentive Models

5. AN OVERVIEW OF INCENTIVE EFFECTS OF WAGES

In Part II we shall continue our investigation of models in which in equilibrium firms pay wages that are higher than the market-clearing wage, so that the market equilibrium is characterized by job queues. In the incentive models of unemployment, if a firm facing an excess supply of labor were to cut its wages, the response of its workers would be so adverse as to outweigh the direct gains to the firm from the lower cost per worker.

To focus on the incentive effects of wages we shall initially assume firms hire from a homogeneous pool of workers, thus abstracting from the adverse selection problems discussed above.

The aspects of behavior that have been most widely discussed as being adversely affected by wages are quitting, quality and intensity of work, and loyalty to the firm.[1] Another way in which wages affect the productivity of individual workers is by affecting whether workers are supportive or antagonistic to their employer. In the economics literature the main contributor to this line of investigation has been George Akerlof in the context of "gift-exchange" relationships. Because there has been little formal modeling of the gift-exchange relationship between employer and employee in the economics literature, we shall only briefly discuss its importance in this introductory section, while reserving most of our efforts in Part II to a discussion of the effect of wages on turnover and on reducing shirking.

This allocation of space should not be interpreted as a judgment on the relative importance of the gift-exchange role of wages compared with the other incentive effects of wages. The indirect effects of wages,

---

[1] The positive effect of high wages on performance has been traced at least as far back as Jacob Vanderlint in *Money Answers All Things*, London 1734. The first modern treatments of the positive effect of high wages on performance were in the context of their effect on reducing quits and were by Steven Salop (1973a,b), and Joseph Stiglitz (1974b).

and wage fluctuations, on effort through their effects on preferences may be as important as the direct effect on quits and shirking of changes in the value of continued employment. However, one of the aims of this monograph is to show that when the assumptions of optimizing behavior by workers and firms are taken seriously and some informational asymmetries are allowed, competitive non-cooperative behavior by firms and workers can lead to unemployment. Consequently, it would be somewhat distracting to show how aspects of behavior (as opposed to aspects of the information structure) that are not usually discussed in conventional models can also lead to unemployment equilibria.

The importance of the goodwill engendered by high wages or the ill-will engendered by low wages can be observed by noting that in most enterprises workers can do significant damage to employers by damaging or causing excessive wear on equipment that is used by many workers, misplacing documents, failing to stop theft or embezzlement, resisting technological (or other) innovations, offending important customers or engaging in other activities that hurt the firm, and are hard for the firm to prevent or detect. Once detected, punishing or even identifying the offender may be difficult if not impossible. Firms must rely on the goodwill of their employees to prevent these harmful actions. Akerlof pointed out that employers voluntarily pay wages to their workers that are higher than would be needed to deter them from quitting. In return, the workers choose actions that are helpful to the employer, and do not choose actions that are harmful. These gifts may also lead workers to stop other employees, customers or suppliers from harming the firm.

It may be possible to induce workers to behave in these desirable ways by combining a high level of supervision with a set of contingency wage contracts. However, even in these cases it may be cheaper for the firm to simply pay high wages and rely on the goodwill of the workers to induce the desired behavior. It also may be difficult to write contracts that foresee all contingencies. For example, if a worker were to sprinkle salt over a pile of printed wiring boards while eating her lunch, she could impose substantial costs on the firm. However, it may be difficult for a personnel officer to foresee this possibility when formulating regulations governing where a worker can eat her lunch. Continuously rewriting these regulations as managers become aware of new possibilities for workers to harm the firm does not appear to be an especially efficient way for the firm to cope with this problem. (The recent surge of successful wrongful dismissal suits on the part of workers seriously limits the power of firms to fire workers for cause when the worker did not violate an explicit rule of the firm.)

Achieving the optimal incentives by paying each worker a wage equal to the value of his (possibly negative) marginal product at the end of each work period, seems equally unrealistic for a large integrated firm in which the marginal product of any worker is almost impossible to measure, and the limited capital of workers precludes employers from having workers bear the full costs of (discovered) harmful actions which they might have taken. These measurement problems and capital market imperfections also limit the usefulness of tournaments (paying workers according to their ranking by productivity among their co-workers). Tournament contracts are also likely to have difficulty in attracting workers since each worker must bear some risk associated with the distribution of workers that the tournament firm attracts. If all firms were offering time rate pay and one firm were to deviate to a tournament pay schedule, workers would be very uncertain about the ability distribution of workers attracted to the tournament firm. This strategy uncertainty could deter applications from all workers. (Even the highest ability types might think that only workers of their ability would be attracted and hence they would be equally likely to rank at the bottom as at the top of the productivity distribution.)

5.1. Employment fees

Another "solution" to the "problem" of job queues persisting in equilibrium is to posit that firms would charge workers an employment fee. This fee would be paid when a worker was initially hired. Ignoring income effects, the initial employment fee would not affect the behavior of individual workers.[2]

As we discussed in Section 1, and as Carmichael [1985] points out, in the absence of sorting and income effects, initial employment fees

---

[2] Indeed, to the extent that both quits and shirking are risky activities (have the possibility of causing income losses), if workers' absolute risk aversion decreases, then by making workers poorer initial employment fees will decrease quits and shirking. Hence, under those circumstances, the income effects of employment fees will make the imposition of those fees more attractive to firms.

could enable the firms to capture the rents accruing to employed workers, and therefore would eliminate job queues. If there were unemployment, a firm could increase its profits by increasing its employment fee (lowering its entry level wage). Its cost per worker would fall without any corresponding increase in its turnover rates or cost of supervision. Again, *modulo* income effects, a worker's decision to quit his firm and his choice of a level of effort, are functions only of the wage he is receiving, the distribution of wages across firms and of the unemployment rate (if some workers quit into unemployment) not of the employment fees. In equilibrium, the availability of employment fees would make workers indifferent among the wage-fee combinations offered by different firms. As in the adverse selection model with testing presented in Section 4, these fees could take the form of low wages paid to newly hired workers.

In Section 1 we presented several arguments against firms selling jobs either through charging employment fees or by requiring workers to work initially for low wages at jobs requiring minimal, or no supervision. Perhaps the most important of those was that bankruptcy and limited capital of workers prevent firms from capturing all the surplus associated with high wage jobs. Selling jobs by requiring newly hired workers to work at low wages during some initial employment period seems reasonable as part of a sorting contract when workers know considerably more about their own abilities than do firms. It seems less reasonable as a means of eliminating job queues generated by the effort inducing effect of high wages. In the latter case it is necessary for there to be some jobs at which firms can make positive profits from unsupervised workers. In addition, assigning high ability workers to low wage jobs at which they are relatively unproductive does not avoid, and may accentuate, the efficiency losses associated with these efficiency wage models. Although, formally, unemployment could be eliminated, as we argued in Section 1, this seems to be more of a semantic than a real change.

5.2. Incentive models

The simplest incentive models are those in which wages affect quit probabilities. Equilibrium may be characterized by a single wage or many wages being offered, with job queues (involuntary unemployment) at all the wages. No firm lowers its wages because, in equilibrium, the increase in its turnover costs from lowering its wage would be at least as great as the reduction in its per hour labor costs from the lower wage. The distribution of wage offers, and the (on the job) search behavior of workers is such that the high wage firms find that their direct cost of offering a high wage is directly offset by the lower probability of a worker quitting. We shall discuss this quit model in Section 6. In Section 7 we discuss the incentive effects of wages and unemployment rates on worker effort. High wages and high unemployment rates each deter shirking and hence reduce supervision costs. Consequently, the unique equilibrium may be one in which firms offer wages at which there is an excess supply of labor. In Section 8 we discuss the direct effect of wages on nutrition and hence on worker productivity. Again, equilibrium may be characterized by unemployment. In that model a more equitable distribution of wealth may also increase output.

6. THE EFFECT OF WAGES ON TURNOVER

In order to show that the quit deterring effect of high wages can generate unemployment, it is necessary to first construct a model in which there are some quits to be deterred. The model we present is an extension of work by Steven Salop and Joseph Stiglitz.

To focus on the incentive effects of wages we shall assume all workers are identical, and that tastes do not change over time. We also simplify the analysis by only allowing a firm to offer a set of wages rather than wages schedules in which wages rise with seniority as in the Salop and Salop [1976] sorting model of quit behavior. We assume throughout that workers quit their jobs if and only if they are offered higher wages elsewhere. (For the reasons discussed in Section 4, we again assume that firms do not match outside offers).

The main results we present in this section are that equilibrium may be characterized by all firms offering the same wage(s) or by each firm offering a different wage. There can be job queues at (almost) every wage. At each wage offered in equilibrium, the gain to a firm from cutting its wage and thus reducing its wage bill is exactly offset by the cost to the firm from the increased turnover induced by this wage cut.

6.1. The economy

We shall focus on the steady state of an economy, in which there are **N** workers and **M** firms. Workers are either employed by firms in the industrial sector or are unemployed—in which case they may engage in household production or other work in the non-industrial sector. The price of the output of goods produced in the non-industrial sector is the numeraire, and production in that sector has constant returns to scale.

To focus on the incentive effects of wages we assume that all workers and firms are identical. For expositional ease we assume that if two firms have the same labor costs they will employ the same number of workers.

The turnover cost to a firm from a quit is **T**. Job changes are costless to workers. The cost of non-labor inputs is fixed. The production technology for firms in the industrial sector is constant returns to scale up to some output level **K**. **K** is sufficiently small that no firm would wish to become a monopsonist in the labor market as a means of becoming a monopolist in the product market.

The price of output in the industrial sector is a decreasing function of total employment in that sector. As employment in the industrial sector goes to zero the price of the output in that sector goes to infinity.

At the end of each period, **bN** workers leave the labor force (the death rate) and an equal number enter the labor force. The probability of exit is independent of the employment status of the worker. At the beginning of the next period, before production begins, firms announce wage offers; workers apply to work for firms; and firms accept some, or all, of their job applicants.

For the purpose of analyzing application decisions of workers, we can consider new entrants and unemployed workers as being self-employed at a wage of **r**. Workers apply sequentially to every firm offering a wage higher than that offered by their present employer (this wage is **r** in the case of the unemployed and new entrants).[1]

The sequence of applications is as follows. All workers first apply for the highest wage job(s) being offered, as long as that wage is higher than the wage they are already getting. Workers that do not get hired at that wage apply to work at the second highest wage job(s) (except for those

---

[1] This assumption differs from the assumption in Section 3 that workers can only apply to one firm. However, in both models we obtain job queues at all but one wage.

workers that are already quitting the second highest wage). This sequence continues until we get to the lowest paid jobs—only the unemployed and new entrants apply to work for those jobs.

Note that we are not analyzing equilibria in which all job changes require an intervening spell of unemployment, as in Salop (1979). Rather we are focussing on on-the-job search. This focus is justified by longitudinal surveys such as the Panel Study of Income Dynamics that find that two-thirds of all job changes that were initiated by a quit are not accompanied by an intervening spell of unemployment.

Hiring occurs immediately after firms make wage offers, but before production begins for the period. The technology is such that all firms must replace all of their workers who quit or retire. There are U unemployed workers, so that if there are no quits the probability of an unemployed worker being hired in a given period is $b(N - U)/[b(N - U) + U]$.

As we shall see, there is, in general, a continuum of equilibria in these models. For any parameter values T, b, N, r, the equilibrium wage determines the level of employment in the industrial sector. Higher wages will be associated with higher levels of unemployment. We shall assume M is large, and ignore integer problems in our computations.

6.2. Single wage equilibria

Let us first analyze equilibria in which all firms offer the same wage, w. If one firm were to deviate and offer a wage $x < w$, it would find that its quit rate was

$$q(x,w) = (1-b) \frac{\dfrac{b(N-U)(M-1)}{M}}{bN + (1-b)U + \dfrac{N-U}{M}}$$

The first term on the right hand side denotes the fraction of the firm's workers that apply for jobs at the higher wage firms: namely, all those that do not retire. The second term gives the ratio of vacancies to applicants for high wage jobs and thus is the probability that a worker that applies to all the high wage firms is hired by one of them.

Note that $q(x,w)$ is a constant for $x < w$ and 0 for $x \geq w$.

From our assumptions that the price of output in the industrial sector is a decreasing function of output in that sector, and that there is constant returns to scale in production, we know U is an increasing function of w, and $\partial q(x,w)/\partial w < 0$.

In this model there generally is a continuum of single wage equilibria, each entailing a different level of unemployment. This is because whenever all firms are offering the same wage, a small wage cut would cause a disproportionately large increase in the firm's turnover costs. There will generally be an interval of wages over which the increase in turnover costs from a wage cut outweighs the gains to the firm from reducing its wage bill. At the relatively high wage equilibria the firms' costs per worker are higher, fewer workers are employed, and output is lowered to the point where the firms earn zero profits.

Starting from a situation where all firms were offering the same wage, if a firm were to deviate, it would always deviate to the reservation wage r: By definition, r is the lowest wage that an unemployed worker would accept.

If the wage offered by all other firms were w, then the wage cut would be deterred if and only if $w - r \leq q(r,w)T$. For w sufficiently close to r this condition is surely satisfied. At these wage levels, there may be unemployment, but no firm would lower its wage since the cost of increased quits at the lower wage would outweigh the labor savings. A firm wouldn't increase its wage since the higher wage would not reduce quits: in the single wage equilibrium, there are no quits. In Figure 9 the interval from r to s describes the range of single wage equilibria. The higher wages in that interval correspond to higher unemployment rates.

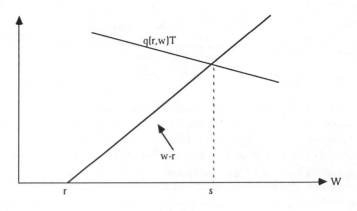

FIGURE 9

If the population were to expand, increasing **N**, then for any wage the number of unemployed workers would increase. If a firm considers dropping its wage from **w** to **r** it would find that the larger the labor pool is the smaller would be the increase in its turnover. Fewer of its workers would be able to succeed in getting jobs with the high wage firms. Thus an increase in the size of the labor force causes a downward shift in the **q(r,w)** function and a fall in the upper support of the range of single wage equilibria.

Similarly, a decrease in the cost of turnover **T** would cause a fall in **q(r,w)** function. However, lower turnover would also cause a decrease in the labor costs of firms, and a concomitant increase in employment and decrease in unemployment which would raise the **q(r,w)** function. Depending on whether the **q(r,w)** function were to rise or fall, the upper support of the distribution of single wage equilibria would increase or decrease.

Finally an increase in the reservation wage from **r** to **r + D** would not affect the **q(r,w)** function outside the interval **r** to **r + D**. The lower limit of the range of single wage equilibria would increase to **r + D**; the upper limit would increase to the intersection of the **q(r,w)** function and the 45° line through **r + D**.

6.3. Multiple wage equilibria in mixed strategies

If firms are of finite size, there can not be a multiple wage equilibrium in pure strategies, where the strategy of a firm is a wage to offer, and a number of workers to hire. Suppose some firms were offering higher wages than others. If the profits of the highest and lowest wage firms were the same, then a firm would increase its profits by switching from being a high wage firm to being a low wage one. Since there would be fewer vacancies at the high wage firms (there is one fewer high wage firm), the quit rate of the low wage firms would fall and the profitability of the low wage firms would increase. Because this deviation increases the profitability of the deviating high wage firm, for a multiple wage equilibrium to exist the profits of a firm offering the highest wage must be strictly greater than the profits of a firm offering the lowest wage. If, however, a firm offering the highest wage were making greater profits than the firm offering the lowest wage, a low wage firm could increase its profits by switching to being a high wage firm; its labor costs would not be affected. Thus a pure-strategy multiple wage equilibrium can not exist if firms have finite size.

 If we allow firms to choose mixed strategies, we can have a multiple wage equilibrium. Let us consider an equilibrium in which the firms mix over two wages L,H, where $L < H$. The quit rate at the low wage firms is a function of the number of workers employed by the high wage firms, as well as the unemployment rate. In equilibrium each firm is indifferent between offering the high and low wage. That is, given the strategies of the other firms, a firm offering wage L would have the same costs per worker as a firm offering H. The cost per worker is the high wage H, and that wage determines the number of workers employed in the industrial sector. We shall consider symmetric mixed strategy equilibria where each firm offers H with probability z and L with probability $1 - z$. Computing the quit rate as the ratio of quits to the number of workers hired at the beginning of the period, the expected quit rate for a firm offering wage L is

$$(1 - b) \frac{zb(N - U)(M - 1)/M}{N - (1 - b) z(N - u)(M - 1)/M}$$

The numerator is the expected number of high wage vacancies at other firms, and is the expected level of employment at high wages by firms other than the firm contemplating offering only wage L, times the attrition rate. The denominator is the number of applicants for these high wage firms: all workers apply for those jobs except those whose current employer offers the high wage H.

To show the existence of a mixed strategy multiple wage equilibrium consider $L = r$, and $H = (r + s)/2$, where r and s take the values shown in Figure 9 for the single wage equilibria of this economy.

For z sufficiently close to 0, the quit rate for a firm offering wage L is also close to zero, and hence low wages are more profitable than high wages.

For z sufficiently close to 1, the high wage firm has lower labor costs than does the low wage firm. This can be seen directly from considering the single wage equilibria described in Figure 9. At $z = 1$ and $L = r$, the cost of the high wage firm and the low wage firm would be equal if $H = s$. For $H = (r + s)/2$, the wage costs to a high wage firm is lower than at $H = s$, and the employment level is higher, hence, the incidence of turnover for a low wage firm is greater than at $H = s$. Consequently, at $z = 1$, $H = (r + s)/2$ and $L = r$, wage H is more profitable than r.

By continuity, there exists a proportion z of high wage firms such that the labor costs of the low and high wage firms are equal when $H = (r+s)/s$ and $L = r$. This argument can be made for every value of H in the interval (r,s). Thus, holding L fixed at r, for every value of H in the open interval (r,s), there is a corresponding value of z such that L,H is a two wage mixed strategy equilibrium. This continuum of two wage equilibria has the curious property that as we increase H from r to s, the values of z needed to support the equilibrium also increase. This is because as we increase H, the labor cost from offering a high wage increases. To make firms indifferent between offering a high and low wage the turnover cost from offering a low wage must increase by an offsetting amount. This can only be done by increasing z, which increases the proportion of firms offering high wages. The increase in z must offset the reduction in turnover caused by the higher wages reducing employment and hence increasing the competition for the available high wage jobs. The "high" wage equilibria have high wages in two senses: the highest wage is relatively high and the proportion of firms offering the high wage is high. Because the cost of labor is higher at the high wage equilibria, those equilibria will also have lower levels of employment.

We can construct other sets of two wage equilibria by moving the low wage in the interval $[r,s)$. At each of these equilibria firms prefer to offer L to r, and the value of z is such that firms are indifferent between offering L and H, where H lies between L and s. It is apparent that there are also mixed strategy equilibria in which firms mix more than two wage offers.

One problem for these and other mixed strategy equilibria is why the indifferent firms choose precisely the mix of strategies needed to sustain the equilibrium. A possible answer could come from an analysis of the evolution of a market in which firms pursue pure strategies. That analysis would let firms that make positive profits grow or propagate. If the distribution of pure strategies approaches a mixed strategy equilibrium, that would provide some grounds for believing that the mixed strategy equilibrium is a useful representation of actual market phenomena. An analysis of that issue is beyond the scope of this monograph.

6.4. Multiple wage equilibria in pure strategies

As we've observed, there cannot be a pure-strategy multiple wage equilibrium when firms have finite size. Let us now consider the case in which the number of workers hired by each firm is infinitesimally small, so that each firm ignores the effect of its wage decisions on the aggregate turnover rate. In particular, it seems reasonable to argue that in most (all?) competitive labor markets a high wage firm would not be induced to become a low wage firm by the effect its *own* wage cut would have on the turnover rates of the low wage firms. Although eliminating one high wage firm (itself) reduces the quit rate of the low wage firms, this effect is unlikely to be of sufficient magnitude to affect the decisions of the firm. The way we shall model a labor market in which changes in the wage offers of a single firm do not affect the distribution of workers applying to firms offering different wages, is by assuming that no firm hires a finite number of workers.

The economy roughly corresponds in other respects to that described in the previous subsections of this section. The salient features of that economy are as follows. There are constant returns to scale in production (we present our arguments in terms of the numbers of workers hired at each wage). The price of the output of the industrial sector is a decreasing function of employment in that sector. As employment goes to zero the price goes to infinity. Conversely, as labor costs go to infinity, employment goes to zero. In equilibrium the cost per worker at diffent wages is the same: the lower direct costs of the low wage firms are exactly offset by their higher quit rates.

We continue to assume that at the end of each period a proportion b of all workers die, and the same fraction b of new workers enter the labor force. Firms then offer wages that they will pay for the duration of the next period and try to maintain their number of employees. Workers apply to every firm offering a higher wage than their current employer. They go to work for the firm that agrees to hire them at the highest wage. If no firm offers them a higher wage than their current employer they do not quit.

We shall describe the steady state of this economy: firms do not change their wage offers from one period to the next.

We shall begin by discussing a two wage equilibrium. We shall then show how the argument can generalize to a multiple wage equilibrium and to an equilibrium with a continuum of wages. In the two wage equilibrium let l denote the number of workers hired at the low wage L, and h denote the number of workers hired at the high wage H. The quit rate at L is $q(L;l,H,h) = (1-b)bh/(l+U+bh) = (1-b)bh/ (N-(1-b)h)$. In equilibrium no firm has an incentive to change its wage offer. Thus:

$$L + q(\cdot)T = H,$$

or h is such that

$$(1-b)bhT/(N-(1-b)h) = H - L. \tag{6.1}$$

and

$$r + bT + \frac{(1-b)bhT}{N-(1-b)h} + (1-b)\left[1 - \frac{bh}{N-(1-b)h}\right]$$

$$\left[\frac{bl + \dfrac{(1-b)lbh}{N-(1-b)h}}{N-(1-b)l-h}\right]T \gtreqless$$

$$L + bT + \frac{(1-b)bht}{N-(1-b)h}$$

or, rearranging terms,

$$\frac{(1-b)(N-h)NblT}{\{[N-(1-b)h]^2[N-(1-b)l-h]\}} \geqq L - r. \tag{6.2}$$

(6.1) ensures us that no wage in the open interval (L,H) generates higher profits to a firm than does wage H, and that wage L generates the same profits as H. (6.2) ensures that no wage in the interval $[r,L)$ generates higher profits than does wage L. Since there are not quits at wage H, we know that firms offering wages above H have strictly greater costs per worker than firms offering wage H. We shall assume that competition in the product market is such that in equilibrium all firms break even. Thus a firm offering a wage greater than H would generate losses.

Letting $L^d(H)$ denote aggregate labor demand when labor costs are H, by definition $\{H,h,l\}$ must satisfy

$$L^d(H) = l + h \tag{6.3}$$

Finally, for l and h workers to be hired

$$l + h \leq N \tag{6.4}$$

To show that these conditions can hold, note that for h equal to zero the left hand side of (6.1) is equal to zero, and hence is less than the right hand side. For **h** equal to **N** the left hand side of (6.1) is equal to (1 − b)T. Hence if the difference between the wages is less than the expected per worker cost of quits to the low wage firm, the left hand side of (6.1) would exceed the right hand side. Consequently, for any values of **H** and **L** such that **H** − **L** < T(1 − b), there exist employment levels at **H** for which the labor costs at **H** and **L** are equal.

Equation (6.2) can certainly be satisfied by choosing **L** = **r**. For **L** in the interval [r,s) in Figure 9, (6.2) will also be satisfied. Thus, there is an interval of "lowest" wages that can support a two wage equilibria. For each of the wages in this interval, there will usually be a continuum of two-wage equilibria. Indeed, there will, in general, be a continuum of **n** wage equilibria, where **n** is any finite number.

In particular for **L** = **r** and each value of **H** < **T** + **r**, there is a corresponding value of **h** satisfying (6.1).

If that **H**,**h** pair satisfies **h** < L^d(**H**) ≦ **N**, (6.3) and (6.4) are also satisfied. Then the wages and employment levels described comprise an equilibrium with **l** = L^d(**H**) − **h**. Holding **L** fixed at **r**, there are, in general, a continuum of values of **H** and **h** that support an equilibrium two wage distribution.

This result does not depend on holding **L** fixed at **r**. We could have made a similar argument for any wage in the interval [r,s).

No high wage firm would lower its wage to a level between **L** and **H**, because the increase in its quits would outweigh the reduction in its wages. No firm would lower its wage to **L**, because that wage cut would not increase the firm's profits. Wage offers slightly below **L** would be less profitable than wage offers at **L**, because the increase in quits would outweigh the benefit to the firm from lower wages.

For each two-wage equilibrium, the higher is the value of **H**, the greater is the cost of labor (the cost of labor must be the same at all the wages offered at any equilibrium), and consequently the higher is the unemployment rate.

Let us now consider the three wage equilibria. We label the wage offers **X** < **L** < **H** and the corresponding employment levels at each of those wages **x**, **l** and **h** where, **X** = **r**, and **L**,**l** and **x** are chosen so that (6.2), with the variable appropriately relabeled, holds as an equality. Given that value of **L**,**H** and **h** are chosen such that (6.1) holds as an equality. The derived level of **H** then dictates the cost of labor in the industrial sector and thus the employment level in that sector. This aggregate level of employment is satisfied through the appropriate choice of **x**.

As we discussed for the two-wage case, there is a continuum of three wage equilibria. The lowest wage need not be equal to **r**. The lowest wage must merely be close enough to **r** that deviations from the lowest wage to **r** do not increase the deviating firm's profits by an amount sufficient to outweigh the firm's increased quit rate from choosing a lower wage.

Clearly the analysis presented for the two and three wage equilibria can be extended to equilibria with any finite number of wages being offered. In any equilibrium in which more than one wage is being chosen, employment levels at all but the lowest wage are determined by the wage distribution, so the wage distribution must be such that aggregate labor demand exceeds those employment levels. In the two wage case we had to concern ourselves only with employment at the highest wage.

We've been careful to limit the discussion of pure-strategy multiple wage equilibria to infinitesimally small firms. The reason the analysis does not go through when firms are large is that a high wage firm could switch to being a low wage firm; this action lowers the quit rate of low wage firms. Hence, if high and low wage firms initially made the same profits, a large high wage firm could always increase its profits by becoming a low wage firm. With finite sized but small firms the equilibria described in this subsection would be approximate or epsilon equilibria. That is, as the proportion of the labor force employed by each firm goes to zero the gain to a firm from deviating from any of the equilibria we've described goes to zero. This is apparent since a firm's wage(s) has an effect on the quit rates of lower wage firms that is proportional to the firm's size.

7. EFFORT INDUCING EFFECTS OF WAGES

7.1. Introduction

Effort models are similar to the quit models expounded in Section 6. In both the quit and effort models wages and unemployment rates affect the behavior of workers in ways that matter to the firm. High wages and high unemployment rates reduce quits and increase effort. Similarly, in both models, if workers could be made to put up sufficiently large bonds, there would be no need to use wages to affect behavior. Since these bonds would eliminate quits and shirking at the Walrasian wage these models would not generate involuntary unemployment.

The most influential wage incentive models, such as Lazear [1979, 1981], Shapiro and Stiglitz [1984], and Bulow and Summers [1986], assume that firms pay a single wage for the entire employment history of a worker, and that workers do not put up a performance bond, a lump sum payment to the firm at the time they are hired. We shall discuss the importance of the single wage assumption at some length in the latter part of this section.

The rationale for not allowing performance bonds has already been discussed. While the arguments against performance bonds have some validity, one would expect that the profit maximizing contract would entail some (albeit limited) performance bonding. On the other hand, we would not expect performance bonding to eliminate the inefficiencies customarily generated by efficiency wages.

The one important difference between the quit averting and effort inducing effects of wages is that when wages are chosen to deter shirking the rigor of supervision as well as the standards imposed by the firm for a worker to keep his job are critical choice variables of the firm. In an effort model the cost of supervision affects both the wage and the equilibrium unemployment rate. If perfect monitoring were sufficiently cheap, firms could pay wages that were arbitrarily close to the reservation wage of their workers and still deter shirking. (By perfect monitoring we mean monitoring that is continuous and precise.) At the risk of some abuse of language, we shall use the precision of a monitor to refer to the error with which performance or effort is measured—if performance is measured without error, then we call that measurement precise.

In more traditional economic models each worker receives a wage which, when combined with the non-wage benefits and costs of the job, makes him indifferent between that job and his best alternative opportunity, which could be another job, or leisure. The cost of the job includes the disutility of the effort demanded by the firm. Of course, for the level of effort demanded by the firm to have any force—to affect the utility of the job or the performance of the worker—effort must be directly or indirectly monitored. Let n denote the level of effort demanded by the firm. If the compensation paid, C^* were to make the worker indifferent between continued employment with the firm at effort level n and becoming unemployed, and if the worker's desired level of effort was less than n, then the worker would only put out the demanded level of effort if he were continuously and precisely monitored. (Continuous monitoring is needed for a test to be accurate.) This is because workers are indifferent between continued employment and being fired at effort level n, but gain some positive surplus if they work at a lower effort level $\mathbf{n}^\# < n$. The positive surplus they gain is equal to the difference in the utility they gain from effort level $\mathbf{n}^\#$ versus n times the probability of a worker contributing effort level $\mathbf{n}^\#$ not being detected shirking when effort n is being demanded.

For our purposes let a contract describe a wage and a level of observed effort below which the workers would be fired. If monitoring were imprecise, so that effort were observed with error, then contract $\{\mathbf{C}^*, n\}$, would induce the worker to contribute a level of effort below n. This result holds whether or not effort is continuously monitored.

7.2. Precision of monitoring

If effort were randomly observed, but the observations were precise (so that whenever effort was measured the firm knew exactly what the effort level was), and the utility of workers was everywhere decreasing in effort,[1] then contract $(\mathbf{C}^*, n)$ would induce workers to contribute no effort. The workers would gain the surplus associated with a wage of $\mathbf{C}^*$ and zero effort until they were monitored and fired. Thus even if a contract such as $\{\mathbf{C}^*, n\}$ were taken by a worker, that worker would gain some positive surplus from the job unless monitoring was both continuous and precise.

Note that when the labor contract is $\{\mathbf{C}^*, n\}$, and monitoring is not continuous, *errors* in the firm's observation of worker effort could *increase* the effort of workers. The reason is that without measurement error, a worker that chooses to contribute less than the contractually demanded level of effort would choose zero effort. Since the worker is indifferent between employment and unemployment when contributing n of effort at wage $\mathbf{C}^*$, and because monitoring is not continuous, the worker is strictly better off contributing zero effort.

---

[1] In the notation presented below this corresponds to $\mathrm{n}^* = 0$.

With precise monitoring, workers also choose less than n of effort. However, because workers prefer continued employment at contract $\{C^*, n\}$, which induces less than n of effort, to becoming unemployed, the worker may choose a positive level of effort to decrease the probability of being fired when monitored. In particular, if the marginal disutility of effort is zero at an effort level of zero, then the worker facing imprecise monitoring would always choose a positive level of effort.

Since the effort of supervisors determines the accuracy and precision with which the effort of workers is monitored, unless supervisors are given contracts that induce continuous and precise monitoring, contract $\{C^*, n\}$ will induce workers to contribute less than n of effort. However, if all workers, including supervisors, are paid wages that make them indifferent between staying with the firm and being fired, continuous and precise monitoring of low level workers would require continuous and precise monitoring of every level of supervision above them. Thus perfect monitoring in these traditional models is likely to impose greater costs on the firm than a wage system with imperfect monitoring that gives a worker rents that the worker loses if he is fired for poor performance.

In general, a wage-supervision system that relies solely on perfect monitoring to induce a given level of effort, n, is dominated by a wage-supervision system that combines a penalty from being fired (induced by the rents paid to continuing employees) with some (imperfect) monitoring. These rents could be a combined consequence of wages that are greater than the lowest wage needed to contribute the contracted level of effort, of imprecise monitoring that may induce workers to contribute less than the contracted level of effort, and of infrequent monitoring which would lead workers to shirk. In particular if the contract were $\{C^*, n\}$ and if monitoring is imprecise, then workers will choose a level of effort between 0 and n. If monitoring is precise, but inaccurate, then workers will choose a zero level of effort. For contract $\{C^*, n\}$, effort is not monotonic in the precision of the monitoring. If monitoring is sufficiently imprecise it will also induce levels of effort near zero.

If the contract were such that a worker strictly preferred employment at the mandated level of effort to unemployment, imprecise monitoring could lead the worker to contribute more than the mandated level of effort. However, the extreme results would still hold: sufficiently imprecise monitoring would induce levels of effort arbitrarily close to zero.

7.3. Allowing positive utility of effort

Of course, independent of compensation workers may prefer some positive level of effort to contributing no effort. We shall assume that only above some level of effort, denoted by n^*, do workers dislike additional effort.[2] To simplify the exposition we also assume that a worker's utility level is separable in income and effort, so that n^* is independent of the level of compensation paid to the worker, and that utility is differentiable at n^*, so that $\partial U(C,n^*)/\partial n = 0$. Finally, we assume that output is linear in the effort supplied by workers, and that output prices are fixed. We choose the units of effort so that output is equal to effort.

We shall show that if monitoring is costly, the firm may only demand n^* of effort. This is true even if monitoring costs go to zero as the frequency with which effort is monitored goes to zero. In analyzing this problem we let the choice variables of the firm be a level of effort n required, a level of compensation C to be paid, and a probability p of monitoring effort in any period. To focus on the effect of a non-monotonic relationship between utility and effort, we shall assume that whenever a worker's effort is monitored it is measured precisely.

Consider a firm demanding n^* of effort and paying compensation of C^* when C^* is the minimum compensation needed to attract workers when workers can choose their own level of effort. That firm would not incur any monitoring costs. Suppose a firm demanded a level of effort $n^\# = n^* + \mu$ and increased the compensation of its workers to $C^\# =$

---

[2] George Akerlof has made the interesting point that n^* is endogenous, and is affected by the wages paid to all workers in the firm. In the absence of monitoring, a worker who feels that he and his co-workers are being fairly treated would wish to work harder than would a worker who feels that managers are treating workers unfairly. Similarly, peer pressure can affect the disutility of effort for individual workers. In firms where workers are ostracized by their peers for rate-busting, the disutility of effort is greater than in firms where high performing workers are lauded by their co-workers for their efforts. Wilfred Brown, in *Piecework Abandoned*, explains the abandonment of piece rate pay schemes as due in part to peer pressure not to exceed the standard rate. We shall largely ignore these important sociological phenomenon and concentrate on the purely economic incentives to work hard.

$C^* + \beta\mu$. Given $C^\#$ there is a minimum probability of being monitored that would induce workers to contribute effort $n^\#$. That is, workers having this compensation contract would contribute $n^\#$ of effort only if the firm were to expend some resources on monitoring effort. We shall show that the profit maximizing strategy for a firm might be to not monitor its workers, even if monitoring costs are continuous at zero monitoring. In particular, we show that, evaluated at $\mu = 0$, as a firm increases μ, the amount of effort demanded, it must also increase the probability of monitoring effort. Thus if monitoring is sufficiently costly, firms may still choose not to demand levels of effort above n^*.

We assume that in each period a worker is paid the agreed upon level of compensation whether or not he is observed shirking (thus we avoid the two sided moral hazard problems of firms cheating). At the end of the period workers that were detected shirking are fired. We assume that there are no hiring costs of workers, that workers' departures from the labor force follow a constant hazard rate and that all workers are identical. Therefore equilibria that are supported by threats to fire workers that are detected shirking are subgame perfect.

Consider a firm offering a contract $\{C^\#, n^\#\}$. Because we've assumed monitoring is precise, workers will either contribute n^* or $n^\#$ of effort. Contracts that *induce* n^* of effort are equivalent to contracts that pay the same compensation and *require* n^* of effort. Thus without loss of generality we can restrict ourselves to contracts that elicit the contracted level of effort.

$V_t(C,n)$ denotes the expected lifetime income of a worker employed at contract $\{C,n\}$ in period t. From the definition of C^* and the assumption that each worker's probability of exiting from the labor force is a constant hazard rate we know the expected lifetime income of a worker employed in period t at contract $\{C^*, n^*\}$, which we denote $V_t(C^*, n^*)$, is equal to the lifetime expected utility of a worker entering unemployment in period t. $U(C,n)$ denotes the one period utility derived from compensation C and effort n. Therefore, for a worker to be deterred from shirking in period t, $C^\#$, $n^\#$ and p must satisfy:

$$U_t(C^\#,n^\#) + V_{t+1}(C^\#,n^\#) \geq U_t(C^\#,n^*) + pV_{t+1}(C^*,n^*) + (1-p)V_{t+1}(C^\#,n^\#) \quad (7.1)$$

or

$$[U_t(C^\#,n^*) - U_t(C^\#,n^\#)]/[V_{t+1}(C^\#,n^\#) - V_{t+1}(C^*,n^*)] \leq p \quad (7.2)$$

(Recall that p was defined as the probability that workers who shirk would be detected shirking.) We shall assume for simplicity that the departure rate of workers from the labor force is a constant hazard rate. Clearly a profit maximizing firm will choose p such that (7.2) holds as an equality.
From (7.2) and using l'Hôpital's rule, we can immediately see that

$$\lim_{\mu \to 0} p = 0. \tag{7.3}$$

However, to determine whether increases in required effort will force the firm to incur monitoring costs, it is necessary to know the value of $dp/d\mu$ evaluated at $\mu = 0$.

Differentiating equation (7.2) with respect to μ, letting N and D respectively represent the numerator and denominator of the left hand side of (7.2), and suppressing the time subscripts.

$$\lim_{\mu \to 0} \partial p / \partial \mu = - U_2/D - N(\beta V_1 + V_2)/D^2 \tag{7.4}$$

where U_1, and U_2 are the derivatives of utility with respect to compensation and effort respectively evaluated at $\{C^*, n^*\}$. V_1 and V_2 are the derivatives of lifetime utility with respect to the per period compensation and effort levels.

Using l'Hôpital's rule, and making use of the fact that $\lim_{\mu \to 0} N = D = 0$, $U_2 = 0$ $V_2 = 0$, and the additive separability of the utility function.

$$\lim_{\mu \to 0} \partial p / \partial \mu = - U_{22}(C^*, n^*)/\beta V_1(C^*, n^*) \tag{7.5}$$

where $U_{22}(C^*, n^*)$ is the second derivatives of utility with respect to effort, evaluated at n^*. From the definition of n^*, we know $U_{22}(C^*, n^*)$ is negative.

Thus, given our assumption that output is linear in effort and normalizing the value of output at one, for a small value of μ an increase in demanded effort changes the profit of the firm by,

$$(1 - \beta) - (dG(p)/dp)dp/d\mu = (1 - \beta) + (dG(p)/dp)U_{22}/\beta V_1 \tag{7.6}$$

where $G(p)$ is the cost to the firm of monitoring workers with an intensity that detects shirking with probability p. Since U_{22} is negative, if the marginal cost of monitoring, $dG(p)/dp$, is sufficiently large, there will be no values of β between 0 and 1 for which (7.6) is positive. In that case increasing the required level of effort around $n = n^*$ would decrease the profits of the firm. This is because demanding more effort forces the firm to incur greater monitoring costs. If monitoring is costly and if $dp/d\mu$ is large, because in order to deter shirking the rigor of monitoring increases rapidly with the amount of effort demanded, these costs will outweigh the benefits to the firm from the greater efforts of its workers. As opposed to $n^* = 0$, if n^* is strictly positive the production process does not preclude n^* from being the effort required by the profit maximizing contract.

Of course, for the profit maximizing contract not to require more effort than the worker would voluntarily contribute not only must (7.6) be negative, but the firm must make non-negative profits at $\{C^*, n^*\}$, and $\{C^*, n^*\}$ must be the globally optimal contract for the firm. In general, these conditions are likely to be satisfied only if there are strong social, or legal pressures causing n^* to be at a high level, or if the work is of sufficient inherent interest as to induce high levels of effort independently of monetary rewards or punishment.

For the remainder of this section we shall assume that those conditions do not all hold, so that firms offer compensation packages and demand levels of employment that make their employees strictly prefer continued employment to becoming unemployed.

To show the most important implications of effort inducing models, we shall first present the broad outline of the Shapiro and Stiglitz [1984] model, the best known of these models. We shall then derive the implications of that model and of the closely related model by Bulow and Summers.

7.4. The Shapiro and Stiglitz wage incentive model

Consider an economy with N identical infinitely lived workers. There is a large number of firms in an industrial (wage) sector. Each firm has a capacity limit k, where k is sufficiently small that a firm would never wish to hire all the workers as a means of becoming a monopolist in the product market. Workers are either employed in the industrial sector or are unemployed (some unemployed workers may be performing household tasks or in other ways be self employed, or may be consuming leisure). Let $U(x)t$ denote the value to the unemployed of being unemployed for a short time period t; x is the value in monetary equivalents of the per period leisure consumed, plus the income equivalent of household production, plus the value of unemployment compensation.

A worker employed in the industrial sector receives a wage **w**. We follow Shapiro and Stiglitz in assuming that workers either shirk or work. Each worker has a von Neumann–Morgenstern utility function that is additively separable in the wage received **w** and labor effort expended **n**. We can normalize the disutility of effort so the utility of a worker is $U(w) - n$; where $\partial U/\partial w > 0$, $\partial^2 U/\partial w^2 < 0$, and $n = 1$ if a worker is not shirking and $n = 0$ if the worker is shirking. Thus we are assuming $n^* = 0$.

Workers can neither borrow nor save. Each worker has an exogenous and constant separation rate **q**. (This assumption is required to ensure that in the steady-state equilibrium some unemployed workers are hired. In a more complicated model with an exogenous arrival rate of new workers and departure rate of old workers this assumption would not be needed.) If a worker shirks there is an instantaneous probability d that the shirking is detected; i.e. as the length of time t during which the worker is monitored becomes small the probability of shirking being detected approaches td. To simplify the notation, define $b = d + q$. The expected life-time utility of a worker who has just been fired is denoted by V_u, and the expected life-time value of employment to a worker who shirks when employed is denoted by $V_{e,s}$. The instantaneous discount rate of workers is denoted by r. Finally assume that workers who are detected shirking are fired.

Consider a worker who is always shirking, and divide the time horizon into short periods of length t. The value of $V_{e,s}$ satisfies the following recursive equation:

$$V_{e,s} \approx U(w)t + \frac{1}{1 + rt}[btV_u + (1 + bt)V_{e,s}] \qquad (7.7)$$

The first term is the utility during the period of length t, the second is the expected utility for all future periods. It is equal to the discounted value of the sum of the expected utility of becoming unemployed, and the expected utility of keeping the job (conditional on shirking). Multiplying both sides of (7.8) by $(1 + rt)/t$ we find,

$$V_{e,s}\left[\frac{1 + rt}{t} - \frac{1 - bt}{t}\right] \approx U(w)[1 + rt] + bV_u. \qquad (7.8)$$

Taking the limit as t goes to zero,

$$V_{e,s} \approx \frac{U(w) + b}{r + b}V_u \qquad (7.9)$$

The analogous computations show that the expected life-time utility of a worker that does not shirk, $V_{e,n}$ can be expressed as

$$V_{e,n} \approx \frac{U(w) + q}{r + q} V_u \qquad (7.10)$$

Finally, letting "a" denote the instantaneous probability that an unemployed worker re-enters the labor force, the same computations show that the life-time value of being unemployed is equal to

$$V_u \approx \frac{U(x) + q}{r + q} V_u \qquad (7.11)$$

Substituting (7.11) into (7.10) and (7.9), and making the purely expositional assumption that a worker that was shirking (not shirking) before becoming unemployed will shirk (not shirk) when re-employed we find[3]

$$V_{e,s} = \frac{[r+a][U(w)] + bU(x)}{r[r+a+b]} \qquad (7.12)$$

$$V_{e,n} = \frac{[r+a][U(w) - 1] + qU(x)}{r[r+a+q]} \qquad (7.13)$$

For a worker to be deterred from shirking it must be the case that $V_{e,n} \geqq V_{e,s}$, or

$$U(w) \geqq U(x) + \frac{r + a + b}{d} \qquad (7.14)$$

Inequality (7.14) is the no shirking condition in Shapiro and Stiglitz. In the steady state equilibrium, there will be no shirking. The accession rate will equal $Lq/(N - L)$, where L is the level of employment in the economy. Note that if $L = N$ the accession rate would be infinite and hence shirking could only be deterred at an infinite wage. Consequently the only equilibrium entails some unemployment.

This result is a consequence of the assumption that all workers are

---

[3] Since, in equilibrium, a worker is indifferent between shirking and not shirking. $V_{e,n} = V_{e,s}$, and this assumption is not needed. We only make this assumption at this point to ease the exposition.

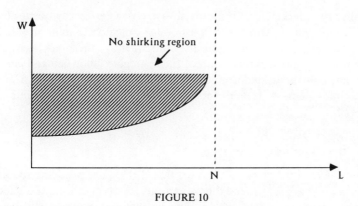

FIGURE 10

identical. If there were heterogeneous workers, then, even under full employment, a worker that was fired would suffer a loss in expected utility due to the adverse signal associated with detected shirking. Consequently, there could be a threat of being fired even with full employment in equilibrium. The threat would depend on the response of firms to the out-of-equilibrium event: a fired worker.

Either a decreasing returns to scale technology, as in Shapiro and Stiglitz or endogenous price formation with a constant returns to scale technology as in Bulow and Summers will give rise to a downward sloping demand schedule (see Figure 11).

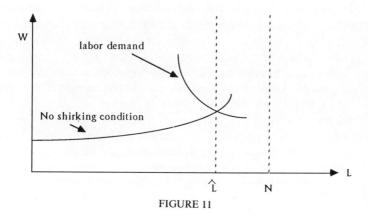

FIGURE 11

Since the market equilibrium is always characterized by queues for wage employment, firms will choose wage contracts to minimize their costs per efficiency unit of labor. Consequently, the market equilibrium will be at the intersection of the aggregate labor demand curve and the no shirking condition as seen in Figure 11. The equilibrium level of employment is $\hat{L}$ and the equilibrium unemployment rate is $(N - \hat{L})/\hat{L}$.

7.5. Differences among workers

From the analysis above we can see that if there are productivity differences across groups, and the two groups are observationally distinct but in other ways identical, the low productivity workers will have longer durations of unemployment. The logic is fairly straightforward. In equilibrium the high productivity workers receive a wage of w_h and have an accession rate (when unemployed) that makes them indifferent between working and shirking. In equilibrium the low productivity workers must receive a wage of $w_l < w_h$ reflecting their lower productivity. Holding all other parameters fixed across the two groups, if the low productivity workers had the same expected duration of unemployment (accession rate) as the high productivity workers, this lower wage would induce the low productivity workers to shirk. Those workers would only be hired when their expected duration of unemployment is sufficiently greater than that of the high productivity workers that they would not be induced to shirk.

The Shapiro and Stiglitz model also suggests that, holding observed productivity fixed, groups for whom turnover from non-shirking related causes is high, will have longer expected durations of unemployment. As we saw above, this is because the expected productivity of a worker determines the worker's wage in the Shapiro and Stiglitz model. But a higher exogenous probability of quitting makes the worker more likely to shirk. Hence those workers would only be deterred from shirking by having a lower accession rate. To the extent that older workers are more likely to retire than are average workers, this theory could explain why, in equilibrium, those workers have longer than average durations of unemployment once unemployed.

A similar explanation for the high unemployment durations of older workers is that they have a high value of leisure relative to their productivity, thus making it more difficult to deter them from shirking. An empirical implication of Lazear [1979] is that for workers near retirement the difference between the value of their output and their value of leisure is likely to be low.

A third explanation for the high durations of unemployment of older workers relies on the importance of contingency contracts for motivating workers. Since older workers are nearer to retirement, firms are more limited in the set of contingency contracts they can offer older workers. Stiglitz and Weiss [1983] showed that the importance of being able to base payoffs on past performance may cause some older workers to be unemployed while all younger workers are hired. They derived this result assuming that the reservation wages of the older and younger workers are the same and that the older workers are *more productive* than the younger ones. Rogerson [1983] has shown that, in general, the optimal contract in a principal agent relationship will involve basing payoffs at the end of any one period on performance in previous periods.

For all these reasons firms may have difficulty inducing the optimal level of effort from older workers.

Similarly, among workers with the same productivity levels, those workers with higher time discount rates, greater disutility of effort, or better alternative opportunities in household employment are more likely to shirk holding the wage and unemployment rate fixed. Since, in equilibrium all workers with the same productivity receive the same wage, the wage-incentive model predicts that in equilibrium those workers will have longer durations of unemployment once unemployed. "Firms prefer to give jobs to workers who 'really need them'".[4] The wage-incentive approach to labor markets would maintain that this "discrimination" in hiring is due, not to altruism or prejudice, but to profit maximizing behavior.

7.6. Effects of unemployment compensation

Shapiro and Stiglitz also consider the effects of unemployment compensation on wages and on the unemployment rate. They find, not surprisingly, that the larger unemployment compensation is the larger will be both in the equilibrium level of unemployment and the equilibrium

---

[4] Bulow and Summers [1986].

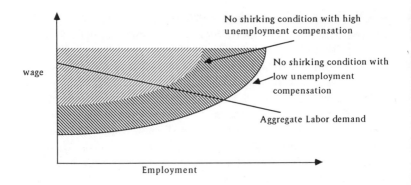

FIGURE 12

wage. Because the monetary loss from being fired is lowered by the amount of unemployment insurance, to deter shirking either the wage paid or the average duration of unemployment must rise. In the Shapiro and Stiglitz model both rise. This is because the equilibrium wage and level of employment occurs at the intersection of the no shirking constraint and the downward sloping labor demand curve. Movements of the no shirking constraint result in movements along the labor demand curve. Hence an increase both in the wage and the unemployment rate is associated with a decrease in employment, and conversely. Thus, if an increase in unemployment compensation does not cause movements in the labor demand curve, it would result in an increase in the wage and in the unemployment rate. From Figure 12, it is also clear that the more elastic is the demand for labor the greater is the effect of a change in unemployment compensation on the unemployment rate. (If monitoring were imprecise, then, depending on the supervision technology, an increase in unemployment compensation could also cause a decrease in the equilibrium level of effort. If this decrease in effort caused a sufficiently large fall in labor demand, the equilibrium wage could fall in response to an increase in unemployment compensation.)

7.7. Macro-economic implications

The effects of *macro-economic* changes on the no shirking condition and hence on the wage, and supervision and effort levels within a firm are less clear.[5] To the extent that an increase in the aggregate unemployment rate causes workers to believe that they are more likely to be fired in the future, it will be more difficult to deter shirking: the no shirking condition would tend to rise. On the other hand, a higher unemployment rate will typically decrease the probability of an unemployed worker finding a job. Hence, an increase in the unemployment rate would increase the penalty associated with being fired and cause a fall in the no-shirking condition. If the second effect dominates then the effort inducing effect of wages would tend to work toward dampening business cycles. If the first effect dominates, the effort inducing effect of wages would tend to accentuate business cycles as firms respond to business downturns by raising wages and respond to upturns by decreasing wages.

The evidence concerning whether the behavior of real wage is cyclical, counter-cyclical or acyclical is mixed. Recent studies by Coleman [1987], Bils [1988], and Moffitt, Keane and Runkle [1987], among others use micro-economic data to correct for changes in the composition of workers over the business cycle, and find only a weak pro-cyclical behavior of real wages. This evidence suggests that the two effects are roughly equal with a slight edge to the second effect—during slumps it is easier to deter shirking, hence wages fall. On the other hand, some studies using macro-economic data find counter-cyclical wage fluctuations. Studies of the cyclical effect of real wages appear quite sensitive to the sample period: during the depression of the early 1930s real wages rose quite dramatically, while during both the slumps of the 1970s and early 1980s and the recovery in the middle and late 1980s real wages have fallen. The fall in real wages during the 1970s seems likely to have been due to the rise in oil prices during that period. It may be that supply induced price changes have different effects than demand induced ones. Hence, any studies of deviations of real wages from trend are likely to be sensitive to the sample years chosen. Because the micro data sets used in studies of the cyclical behavior of wages do not include data from the 1930s, studies that rely on those data sets to correct for compositional changes over the cycle may be misleading.

---

[5] These shocks may also affect the labor demand curve. However, to focus on the macro-economic implications of the incentive model we shall hold the labor demand curve fixed.

The wage-incentive model has also been used by Bulow and Summers to explain large wage increases in industries that are suffering severe declines in employment. (This phenomenon has been documented by C. Lawrence and R. Lawrence (1985)). Bulow and Summers point out that to deter shirking when layoff probabilities are high, it would be necessary to increase wages.

Of course, to the extent that workers have specific skills associated with these declining industries, the fall in employment in these industries would also cause a fall in the accession rate of workers in those industries, thus offsetting the need to raise wages.

The wage incentive models would be consistent with the following wage pattern in a declining industry. The initial effect from a fall in demand would be a fall in the accession rate of roughly the same or greater magnitude as the increase in non-shirking related separations. The increase in non-shirking related separations makes it more difficult for firms to deter shirking, while a decrease in the accession rate makes it easier to deter shirking. Because of these offsetting effects, in the first stages of an industry decline we would not expect a dramatic fall (or rise) in wages. If the decline continues and becomes more severe, the accession rate in the industry would fall to zero. At that point further declines in industry employment would affect the non-shirking related separations without affecting industry hires. Thus only in the latter stages of an industry decline would we find wages falling. This theoretical implication of the incentive models is consistent with the evidence gathered by Lawrence and Lawrence.

7.8. Akerlof and Katz extension

One criticism that has been made of the Shapiro and Stiglitz analysis is that unemployment is not necessary to prevent shirking. Instead firms could induce a given level of effort by paying steep wage tenure profiles: back-loading worker salaries as a means of deterring shirking and paying life-time expected wages that make workers indifferent between employment and unemployment. Akerlof and Katz [1986] have challenged this criticism. They show that, if workers do not improve their firm specific productivity while shirking, and if monitoring is imperfect, then the firm optimal wage schedule is not, in general, one that makes a worker indifferent between employment and unemployment. To deter shirking, it will be necessary for firms to pay some surplus to workers, thus generating job queues.

To see the Akerlof and Katz result, let the disutility of effort for a worker be denoted by v, and the probability of being detected shirking again be denoted by p, and the discount rate for workers by r. If the discount rate for the firm is greater than that for the worker, the optimal contract will involve paying a payment upon retirement of v/p and a wage premium in each preceding period of rv/p. Note that not only does this wage payment scheme involve a substantial lifetime wage premium for employment in the sector in which efficiency wages are paid, but it also involves a relatively flat wage-tenure profile. In continuous time with no learning the Akerlof and Katz model generates a flat wage-tenure profile with a blip up at retirement corresponding to retirement pay.[6]

The intuition behind the Akerlof and Katz result is fairly straightforward. (The reader should see their paper for a formal proof.) To deter shirking in the last period v/p must be paid to non-shirkers at the end of that period. However, with discounting that payment wouldn't deter shirking in the next to last period. To compensate for the effect of discounting on the impact of the last period payment for influencing next to last period behavior, an additional payment of rv/p must be paid to workers not observed shirking at the end of the next to last period. Continuing this argument it is clear that at the end of each period, but the last, a premium of rv/p must be paid. This schedule makes a worker indifferent between working and shirking in each period. If the discount rate for workers is larger than that for firms, the wage schedule derived in Akerlof and Katz is the cheapest means of deterring shirking. A wage schedule that shifted some of the payments to workers to later periods would have to increase those later payments by enough to compensate the workers for receiving the payments later.

---

[6] Recent empirical research by Marshall and Zarkin [1987], Abraham and Farber [1987], and Altonji and Shakotko [1987] use panel data to correct for worker heterogeneity and find much flatter wage-tenure profiles than have been estimated using cross-sectional data. These findings have been seriously challenged to the grounds that the turnover function which distinguishes between returns to experience and returns to tenure is either unspecified or does not accurately capture turnover. However, this research admits the possibility that returns to tenure *may* be significantly lower than previously thought.

If the discount rate of firms is larger than that for workers, this shift in compensation would increase the labor costs of the firm.

This argument depends on workers not improving their firm specific productivity while shirking. If the worker's productivity with the firm increased rapidly with experience, irrespective of whether the workers worked or shirked, the optimal policy for the firm might be to offer contracts that do not deter shirking in the early periods of a worker's tenure. In that case, hiring a worker, and knowing the worker would shirk, might be profitable for a firm given that it will benefit in later periods from the firm specific human capital of the worker. If the productivity of new workers is sufficiently low, this strategy will be more profitable than paying the worker a high enough wage to deter shirking in those early periods. Thus, we could find wages rising with tenure. In addition, by paying workers low wages during the early periods of their tenure the firm could eliminate job queues.

Conversely, if workers can only acquire general human capital while working, then firms may not have the need to deter shirking in the early periods of a workers tenure. In that case we would also find wages rising with tenure—not because the firm chooses not to deter shirking in the early periods but because the worker has no incentive to shirk even if not monitored.

We do not need to worry about the increased risk borne by the workers from these peculiarly shaped wage-tenure profiles since, in the Akerlof and Katz model, the lifetime wage resulting from this constrained optimization problem induces an excess supply of labor. Since Akerlof and Katz assume workers are homogeneous, as long as a wage contract attracts workers and deters shirking it is feasible. Thus even when firms can credibly commit themselves to steep wage-tenure profiles, equilibrium in the labor market will not be market clearing.

Akerlof and Katz acknowledge that if workers can provide bonds (pay large sums to "buy" their jobs) their argument falls apart. However, as we've argued above, the amount of capital available to newly hired workers is likely to be small.

8. THE NUTRITION MODEL

In this section we shall consider the most straightforward case in which wages affect behavior: the nutrition models. In these models the productivity of workers is directly affected by their incomes. Better fed workers have more energy and are less likely to become ill. When firms choose levels of compensation to pay workers they take into account the direct effect of compensation on worker productivity. Since these models are concerned with the direct effect of wages on labor endowments they have been presented in the context of labor markets in less developed countries—labor markets for which differences in income available for consumption have the strongest effect on nutrition and health. The analysis below may be viewed as referring primarily to workers in a less developed country.

One could argue that in most less developed countries the prevailing wage purchases sufficient food so that cuts in that wage would not decrease output by an amount sufficient to outweigh the gains to the firm from the reduced hourly wage bill. However, the relevant effect of wages on nutrition, comes from the food and medical care purchased by the *worker*, not his family. Firms cannot prevent workers from sharing some of their compensation with family members that are not employees of the firm. Firms can, of course, make payments in kind to workers: give them cooked meals and free medical care at the work place. And to some extent these forms of payment are done.

Jobs that are so physically demanding that they require workers to consume 5,000 calories per day, may have to pay workers an amount sufficient to purchase 15,000 calories per day so that the worker himself actually purchases 5,000 calories.

One of the principal ways in which the consumption package of a worker may affect the profits of the firm is through illness. Worker's who report to work ill may damage equipment, make defective products that must later be repaired or, in the case of communicable diseases that are prevalent in less developed countries, cause their co-workers to become ill. Even if the only cost of illness is increased absenteeism, Weiss [1988] has shown that for plausible production functions, absenteeism imposes significant costs on the firm. These costs may be substantial even for firms that do not pay workers when they are absent. They are, of course, greater if the worker is paid when absent.

In order to increase the direct impact of their payments to workers on worker performance, often firms pay some of the income of workers in kind rather than cash by providing free or subsidized meals which must be consumed at the place of employment, and by providing free medical care to the workers. These payments are made in kind because the profits of the firm are affected by the worker's share of the consumption of his family and the worker's choice of purchases among food, medical care, and other consumption goods. The firm wishes the worker to consume products that directly increase (or do not decrease) the productivity of the worker.[1] However, payments in kind are costly. It may be cheaper for a firm to pay workers a wage above the market clearing wage than to hire a kitchen staff for all their meals. We shall assume that the cost of making all payments in kind is sufficiently large that at least part of a worker's wage is in monetary terms, and shall focus our attention on the monetary wages received by workers, and on the interaction between the wages firms pay and the productivity of their workers.

The presentation of this section will be to first give a discursive treatment of the main results in this literature. In Appendix B, we present the Dasgupta and Ray [1987] model of the interaction between wage and non-wage income and labor productivity to provide a context in which these results could be more rigorously derived.

As in the previous sections, except in cases where the proofs are exceptionally intuitive, we shall avoid giving formal proofs of results but rather provide heuristic arguments.

In our exposition, we shall rely heavily on the analysis in Partha Dasgupta and Debraj Ray [1986, 1987]. Other useful approaches to the issues discussed below include J.A. Mirrlees [1975]; C.J. Bliss and N.H. Stern [1978a]; and H. Leibenstein [1957].

---

[1] Among high income individuals in developed economies, firms may subsidize membership in health clubs as a means of shifting consumption patterns in ways that increase the productivity of the worker, and reduce company paid medical expenses. Also company subsidized day care and medical care for dependents may help reduce absenteeism. Of course, in developed economies because fringe benefits of this sort are often not taxed the tax incentives for these payment in kind may be more important than their direct productivity enhancing effects. In general, because workers do not take into account the effect of differences in their consumption on firm profits, policies of the firm which affect the consumption pattern of workers can result in Pareto improvements: small changes in a workers consumption bundle, holding real income fixed, has only second order effects on the utility of workers, but first order effects on firm profits. Consequently, when consumption patterns have major effects on worker performance and when consumption patterns are particularly sensitive to relatively small price differences we would expect firms to try to affect relative prices. A potentially fruitful area of research, which is unfortunately beyond the scope of this paper, would be to investigate whether there are systematic differences in relative prices in company stores that can be explained by the effect of different consumption patterns on productivity.

The basic intuition behind all of these models is that better fed workers have more energy and are less likely to be sick. Increasing the wages of the very poor increases their nutrition level. Bliss and Stern [1978b], and Leibenstein [1957] present empirical evidence that increases in the nutrition of workers can sufficiently increase the productivity of those workers to outweigh the cost to the employer of the higher payment to workers.

8.1. The model

We shall assume throughout that all the characteristics of workers are costlessly observed by both workers and firms. As in Sections 6 and 7 this assumption is made, not because we find it reasonable, but to differentiate the results in this section from those derived in Part I where we focused on the effects of asymmetric information. We also distinguish this model from those presented in Sections 6 and 7 by assuming that quits are exogenous and that effort can be costlessly supervised. Thus the performance of the worker is a function solely of his wage, not of the distribution of wages offered by other firms, nor of the unemployment rate as in those sections.

We assume that there is an interior wage w^* that minimizes the firm's cost per unit of labor input. This is the "efficiency wage" discussed in previous sections. Y^* denotes the profit maximizing level of output for a firm paying wage w^*. If the efficiency wage w^* lies above the reservation wage of all workers, and if the supply of labor forthcoming at that wage exceeds the demand for labor, the market equilibrium will be characterized by all firms paying workers w^* and by job queues (involuntary unemployment) at that wage.

At the efficiency wage, a wage cut would so reduce the labor input of its workers that the firm cutting the wage would be worse off. (The reader may recall seeing a proof of this result in Section 2.) Similarly, a monopsonist would choose to offer w^*, since by definition there is no wage that gives a lower labor cost.

Perhaps the most surprising result of the nutrition models is that if, at the efficiency wage, there is an excess supply of labor, so that there are queues for jobs in the industrial sector, a small increase in the non-labor income of workers will cause not only the wage income of workers to fall, but their total income to fall as well.

Before proving this result, we can provide a rough intuition for it. In ·

the nutrition model both labor and non-labor income positively affect effort. If the increase in non-labor income were precisely offset by a decrease in wages, effort would be unchanged. Starting at that lower wage, firms would find that a given cut in wages would have the same effect on effort as previously. However, while previously a small wage cut left the firm's cost per efficiency unit of labor unchanged, now, because that ratio is lower, the same wage cut would lower the firm's cost per efficiency unit of labor. The assumption that the initial equilibrium was characterized by job queues is essential for the analysis. Otherwise, the fall in the cost per efficiency unit of labor from the increase in non-labor income would cause firms to compete for workers by bidding up wages.

To more rigorously demonstrate the results of the nutrition models, we need to make some assumptions, and introduce more notation.

Let us assume that production functions are characterized by decreasing returns to scale, and that the non-labor income of workers is known by the firms, as is the relationship between total income and labor productivity.

Let $q(w + k)$ denote the input into production of a worker with labor income w and non-labor income k. Suppose no workers had any non-labor income, and suppose further that in equilibrium the labor supply constraint is not binding. Then firms will choose an efficiency wage $w = w^*$ to maximize $H = q(w)/w$; i.e. for that worker, w^* is such that

$$w^* q'(w^*) - q(w^*) = 0. \qquad (8.1)$$

Let us now suppose all workers were to gain some non-labor income k. If the labor supply constraint is not binding, firms will now choose an efficiency wage w to maximize

$$H = q(w + k)/w \qquad (8.2)$$

Suppose firms were to pay workers a wage of $w^* - k$ (so that the total income of that worker is unchanged from the first case)

Evaluating dH/dw at $w = \hat{w} - k$
$$\text{sign } dH/dw = \text{sign}\{(w^* - k)q'(w^*) - q(w^*)\} \qquad (8.3)$$

From (8.1) it is clear that (8.3) is negative. Each firm can increase its labor input per dollar by lowering its wage below w^*. Thus, under the appropriate concavity conditions—ensuring that (8.2) has a unique maximum—if there is an excess supply of labor at $w^* - k$, then an increase in the non-labor income of all potential workers from zero to **k** will decrease the total income of each employed worker.

This result holds whether the firm is a monopsonist in the labor market, or a small firm in a competitive labor market.

Although increasing the non-labor income of workers decreases the total income of each employed worker, it does not, in general, decrease the aggregate income of workers; nor does it necessarily decrease the *ex ante* expected income of workers.

Since increasing the non-labor income of workers enables firms to lower their cost per efficiency unit of labor, firms will employ more efficiency units of labor. As we have shown, an increase in the non-labor income of workers causes a sufficiently large fall in the efficiency wage of paid workers that the total income of employed workers falls. Therefore, each worker will contribute fewer efficiency units of labor, and the percentage increase in the number of workers employed will be even greater than the percentage increase in the amount of efficiency units of labor employed. Thus an increase in non-labor income makes workers better off both by increasing their probability of being employed and by increasing their income if unemployed. Depending on the utility functions of workers and the labor demand functions of firms, these two effects may offset the lower income, conditional on being employed, of workers with significant non-labor income.

Furthermore, although a uniform increase in the non-labor income of all workers reduces the income of employed workers, it is *not* necessarily the case that in a society with wealth differences, the richer employed workers are worse off than employed poor workers. Indeed in competitive labor markets both wages and total income are increasing functions of the observed non-labor income of workers.

When workers differ according to their non-labor income (they own different amounts of land) and these differences are observed by employers, equilibrium wages offered by a monopsonist would differ from those offered in a competitive market. Thus we need to analyze those two cases separately. Let us first consider the wages offered by a monopsonist.

8.2. A monopsonistic firm

Suppose a monopsonist were to offer each worker his individual efficiency wage: that wage which minimizes the worker's cost per unit of labor input (recall that workers only differ according to their non-labor income, and this non-labor income is observed by firms). For simplicity let us also assume that non-labor income is a continuous variable, so that no two workers have the same minimum cost per efficiency unit of labor.

If, at these efficiency wages, there is an excess supply of labor, so that the total number of efficiency units of labor the monopsonist would want to hire at these wages does not exceed the labor supply forthcoming at these wages, then the optimal strategy for the monopsonist is to offer each worker that is hired his efficiency wage. Any other wages would increase his cost per unit of labor input.

However, not all workers would be hired. The workers with the highest cost per efficiency unit of labor, at their efficiency wage, would not be hired. Indeed, we can order the types of workers by their minimum cost per efficiency unit of labor. As jobs are made available to workers with higher costs per efficiency unit of labor, effective labor supply increases while the cost of labor also rises, thus decreasing the quantity of labor the firm wishes to hire. The marginal type hired will be such that at their cost per efficiency unit of labor the demand for labor would be equal to the quantity of labor (in efficiency units) supplied by all types with labor costs less than or equal to the cost of the marginal type. Workers with higher costs per efficiency unit of labor would not be employed.[2] Thus workers with large non-labor incomes would be hired before workers with small non-labor incomes.

8.3. Competitive firms

We turn to the case where there are several firms competing for workers. Except for degenerate cases in which the minimum cost per efficiency unit of labor is the same for several groups of workers, competition among firms would preclude more than one type of workers being paid its efficiency wage. The minimum cost per efficiency unit of labor from workers with high non-labor incomes would be lower than the cost for workers with low non-labor incomes. Consequently firms

---

[2] Note that in contrast to the standard monopsony model, or the asymmetric information model presented in earlier sections, the high costs incurred by hiring the marginal workers do not affect the firm's cost of hiring other types. This is because the different types of workers are observationally distinct.

would compete for those workers, bidding up their wages. Among employed workers, wages (and *a fortiori* total income) would be an increasing function of non-labor income. Even though wealthier individuals have lower "efficiency" wages, competitive forces would cause them to have higher wages in equilibrium. In contrast to the monopsony case, almost all employed workers would be paid more than the wage that minimizes their cost per efficiency unit of labor. In equilibrium, this cost would be the same for all employed workers.

8.4. Comparison of outcomes in different labor markets

In common with the monopsony case, when firms compete for workers a worker would only be hired if all workers with greater non-labor incomes than that worker has are also employed. If there are decreasing returns to scale in aggregate production, and the output price is the same in both cases, then the number of workers hired will be greater when the (local) labor market is a monopsony than if it is characterized by competition among firms for workers. In both cases the marginal worker is the worker who, when paid his efficiency wage, has a cost per unit of labor input equal to the value of the output of the last unit of labor employed. However, in the competitive labor market only the marginal worker, one with non-labor income a, is being paid his efficiency wage. All other employed workers with non-labor income greater than a are paid more than their efficiency wage and more than the marginal worker receives. Those workers are more productive than they would be if they were paid their efficiency wages. To see why employment is lower in the competitive labor market than in the monopsonistic labor market, suppose employment were the same in both markets. Then the marginal worker i would be the same, but aggregate output would be greater in the competitive labor market. Given our assumption of decreasing returns to scale in production, the marginal product of worker i would be smaller in the competitive labor market than in the monopsonistic one. Since the wage paid that worker would be the same in both markets, as is the output price, this difference in marginal products is inconsistent with profit maximizing behavior by firms in both markets.

In both the competitive and monopsonistic markets, nearly identical individuals are being treated in distinctly different ways. Individuals with non-labor incomes below, but arbitrarily close, to that of the marginal worker are unemployed and would, if employed at the wage paid the marginal worker, be made strictly better off: the marginal employed worker is being paid her efficiency wage which is, in general, strictly greater than her reservation wage.

8.5. Wealth redistribution

In a competitive labor market a transfer of wealth from some interval of individuals with wealth strictly above a to all individuals whose wealth lies in some small interval $[a-b, a]$, would increase both output and employment. The minimum cost per efficiency unit of labor for the individuals receiving the transfer would fall (as would their efficiency wage). Since the worker with the initial non-labor income a was the marginal employed worker, once the cost per efficiency unit of labor of that worker falls, competitive pressures would cause the wages of all other workers to fall and would lower the cost per efficiency unit of labor of firms. The wages received by workers in the interval $(a, 1]$ would become closer to their efficiency wages. While the output of workers that lost wealth would fall, their output per dollar of wage income would rise, thus lowering the firms' costs and increasing their production. Since output per worker has fallen employment would also increase.

Thus, in the new equilibrium employment (both in efficiency units and in numbers of workers) would increase. For b small all the workers in the interval $[a-b, a]$ would become employed.

This gain in output can be implemented by transfers either from the rich, those with non-labor incomes strictly above a, or by transfers from the poor: those with non-labor income strictly below $a-b$. In most less developed countries marginal workers are generally landless and have no non-labor income, while unemployed workers may have various degrees of debt. In that case the only feasible transfers are from individuals with non-labor incomes above a to individuals with non-labor incomes at or below a.

On the other hand, there are cases in which increasing income inequality would increase output and employment. Consider a completely egalitarian society in which non-labor income is equally distributed across the population. Suppose that if each worker was paid his efficiency wage (given his non-labor income), the cost per efficiency unit of labor would not justify hiring any workers even if aggregate employment were zero. Consequently, the market equilibrium with a completely egalitarian distribution of non-labor income would be characterized by no employment in the industrial sector.

Now consider a transfer of non-labor income to some small subset of the population **K**. Because this increase in the non-labor income of workers in set **K** increases their productivity at every wage their minimum cost per unit of labor input falls. Consequently these wealthier individuals have become more attractive potential employees and firms might find it profitable to employ these workers. If this transfer resulted in employment of those workers, then making the distribution of non-labor income less egalitarian would (starting from the initial condition of zero industrial employment) increase employment and output in the industrial sector.[3]

A similar line of reasoning shows that in very poor countries, countries where per capita non-labor income is low, we would expect the employment rate in the industrial sector to be considerably lower than in poor countries where non-labor income is greater.

Since the results presented in this section can be derived in a general equilibrium setting using the Dasgupta and Ray model, for completeness we shall present the basic features of that model.

Appendix B. The Dasgupta and Ray model

In the Dasgupta and Ray model the economy is characterized by a quantity of land **T**, and a number of potential workers **N**. **N** is large. For simplicity they order people along the unit interval, and set $N = 1$. Within this interval the density of individuals is constant. Each worker has a label z and a quantity of land t(z). The ordering of people is such that t(z) is non-decreasing in z. They assume t(z) is continuous.

The labor input of a worker is an increasing function of his total

---

[3] Of course, it would not be possible to redistribute income from these employed workers to the unemployed, or from firms to the unemployed and affect a Pareto improvement. Taxing the employed would negate the effect of the transfers to them of non-labor income. Taxing the firms would decrease the efficiency wage at which they could profitably employ workers.

income. The economy has only one output, rice, which is produced by land and labor power. The aggregate number of efficiency units of labor employed is denoted by L, and the quantity of rice produced comes from an aggregate production function F(T,L). F is constant returns to scale, with decreasing marginal products to individual factors, and is everywhere twice differentiable. There are many small firms. Markets for land and labor are competitive. Because of the assumption of constant returns to scale in production the number of firms is indeterminate. An individual either works for a firm or is unemployed. The unemployed engage in non-market activities (including begging) which provides a subsistence level of income. The rent on land, in equilibrium, is $r > 0$, where r is expressed in units of rice. The non-labor income of individual z is thus $rt(z)$. Following Dasgupta and Ray assume that job applicants differ only according to their non-labor income. Thus the reservation wage function may be expressed as $s(rt(z))$.

All agents are perfectly informed.

Definition: An equilibrium is a rental rate r, a set of employed workers G, and a wage function w(z), such that no firm could do better by offering a different wage, or rental rate, or by increasing or decreasing the number of workers it hires.

In equilibrium all land is utilized. The marginal product of land is strictly positive, and there is a decreasing marginal product of labor, so that if some land were not utilized, a firm would purchase its use at a rental rate below r and make strictly positive profits.

The wage schedule implies a rate per efficiency unit of labor. No wage is determined for the unemployed since they do not participate in the market economy. In equilibrium there is no wage, at or above their reservation wage, at which firms would wish to hire them.

Let $q(w + rt(z))$ denote the labor input of worker z receiving wage w, w^* denotes the arg min $(w/q(w + rt(z)))$. Let $y(r,z)$ denote $\{w^*/q(w^* + rt(z))$ for $s(rt(z)) < w^*$ and $w(r,z)/q(w + rt(z))$ otherwise. Thus $y(r,z)$ denotes the minimum cost per efficiency unit of labor firms can obtain from worker z. Holding r fixed, $y(r,z)$ is plotted in Figure 13 for the case in which reservation wages are not binding.

Workers in the interval 0 to z_0 are landless, and assuming no debt, have the same reservation wages and the same efficiency wage; $y(r,z)$ is decreasing in z as long as the reservation wage is not binding. Once the reservation wage binds for some z it is binding for all larger z. For those

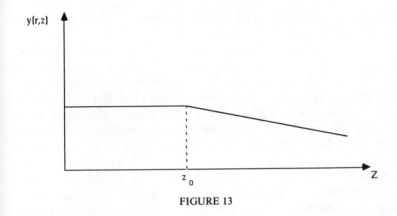

FIGURE 13

values of z for which the reservation wage is binding $y(r,z)$ is not necessarily monotonic in z: there could be alternating regions in which $y(r,z)$
is decreasing and increasing in z.

Given this set-up it is straightforward to prove the results presented
previously in this section.

9. CONCLUDING REMARKS

In this monograph we focused on the sorting, incentive and nutritional
effects of wage contracts to explain why firms may choose not to lower
their wages when faced with an excess supply of labor. We paid less
attention to some of the other explanations that have received recent
attention in the literature.

George Akerlof has stressed the gift-exchange nature of employment
relationships. He argues that when firms pay "high" wages they are in
effect making a gift to the workers, which is reciprocated by the
workers. They act in ways that benefit the firm even if they are not
rewarded for those actions. This gift-exchange model resembles the
Shapiro–Stiglitz (S–S) effort model in that in both cases high wages
induce behavior that benefits the firm. However, in the S–S model high
wages are being paid to increase the threat of being fired. Only anti-
cipated *future* wages and termination probabilities affect the current
behavior of workers. In the gift-exchange model wages affect the

behavior of workers by changing their preferences. The *past* behavior of firms affects the performance of workers.[1]

The two models differ in a variety of other ways as well. The effort model predicts that during periods of high unemployment firms will cut wages, since it is easier to deter shirking when unemployment is high. The gift-exchange model is ambiguous on this issue. During periods of high unemployment firms may even raise wages. For instance when spouses are unemployed the marginal utility of income to a worker is high. Thus, while high wages are more valuable (to the worker) during periods of high unemployment, the "return" to a firm from increasing the value of the gift could also be higher during periods of high unemployment. This could lead firms to raise wages during periods of high unemployment. A more likely outcome would be fairly rigid wages, firms intentionally not "taking advantage" of bad macro-economic conditions to squeeze their workers through lower wages or reduced benefits.[2]

A third source of possible differences would be in the effect of welfare payments. In the effort model higher unemployment compensation is associated with higher wages. This is because unemployment compensation makes it more difficult for firms to deter shirking. In the gift-exchange model unemployment compensation has no effect on wages.

Thus while the effort and gift-exchange models are superficially similar, there are important substantive differences in their empirical and normative content. The gift-exchange model has considerable

---

[1] Note that this asymmetry between workers and firms, where the past behavior of firms affects the preferences of workers but past behavior of workers does not affect the preferences of firms, arises because Akerlof follows the mainstream of economic analysis in modeling firms as profit maximizing entities. In a richer model in which firms were explicitly modeled as coalitions of individuals, past behavior of workers could affect the utility functions of managers and hence induce high current wages irrespective of the incentive or sorting effects of contingency contracts of that sort. Some of the gains from corporate takeovers, and the willingness of raiders to pay premia, may result from new management not feeling an obligation to continue to reward favorable actions that were taken under the previous management. Unfortunately, even a preliminary analysis of factors affecting the preferences and behavior of firm managers vis-a-vis workers is beyond the scope of our work.

[2] The implicit *quid pro quo* for this would be that workers would voluntarily help the firm, perhaps by taking wage cuts when the firm suffers a financial setback during an economic boom.

intuitive appeal and provides useful insights into some employment relationships.

Two other approaches to wage determination that should be mentioned are the insider-outsider models proposed by Assar Lindbeck and Dennis Snower, and rent sharing models. The insider-outsider models are models of wage stickiness. They stress the morale problems caused by replacing experienced workers with newly hired workers that are paid lower wages than experienced workers. In those models experienced and inexperienced workers are complements and firms commit to a lifetime wage when they hire a worker. Thus wages are unresponsive to small macro-economic shocks that would, in more traditional models, result in wage falls.

Rent sharing explanations of wages are based on the proposition that if firms are making high profits, workers have considerable leverage for increasing wages.[3] It is probably more plausible to think of quasi-rents rather than rents as being shared, since the leverage of workers is presumably not lessened by high interest payments by firms.

Evidence

The recent interest in efficiency wage models has been accompanied by research showing significant industry and firm wage differentials. Industry wage differentials seem to persist over time and across countries—high wage industries in one country and time tend to be high wage industries in other places and time periods. These differentials persist after correcting for all characteristics of the workers, including union membership, that are observed by the researcher. However, they are lessened since high wage industries seem to attract workers with characteristics that are correlated with relatively high wages in all industries.

It has been suggested that industry and firm wage differentials provide support for the efficiency wage models, and that by examining the factors correlated with high industry wages we can distinguish

---

[3] There has been a great deal of discussion but very little formal modelling of rent sharing. One of the few rent sharing models is by Wm. Dickens in "Wages, Employment, and the Threat of Collective Action by Workers," NBER #1856, [1986] where the threat of unionization is greater for more profitable firms and hence leads them to pay higher wages.

between the various efficiency wage models. The principal factors associated with high wages are high capital/labor ratios, high profit rates, large firm size, and (as mentioned) a highly qualified work force. Steep wage-tenure profiles seem to be associated with higher wages (Lazear and Moore, 1984). In the fast food industry company owned stores pay higher wages than do franchisees (Krueger, 1989).

Unfortunately, these data do not allow us to reject any of the efficiency wage models. For instance shirking, absenteeism, quits or low ability are all likely to be more costly for firms with high capital/labor ratios or high operating profits per worker. Consequently, the incentive, sorting, and gift-exchange models would all predict high wages in those industries. The rent sharing model also predicts that workers in those industries would have higher wages; in that model it could be due to the greater leverage they have over their employer either through a union or their threat to unionize.

Similarly, the positive correlation between the slope of the wage-tenure profile and expected lifetime wages is consistent with either the effort model or the sorting model. Firms for which high effort and low quit rates are more valuable would tend to offer contracts with steep wage-tenure profiles. Since these contracts distort the actions of the workers, for example they choose more effort than they would with a flatter wage-tenure profile holding expected wages fixed, firms offering these steep wage-tenure profiles would have to offer higher expected lifetime wages to attract workers.

Sorting models with tests predict that workers employed with steep wage-tenure profiles are both more able according to unobserved characteristics and are likely to have passed various internal tests in the firms (Guasch and Weiss, 1980, 1981, 1982). In those models workers with steep wage-tenure profiles have higher wages.

As mentioned, it has been observed also that workers in industries that pay high wages, after correcting for observable characteristics, have observable characteristics such as more education, that are normally associated with higher productivity (or at least higher wages). Consequently, one might think that workers in those industries are likely to also have better unobserved characteristics. This evidence provides some support for sorting explanations of inter-industry wage differentials.

One observation that almost all models of the labor market have difficulty explaining is why industry wage differentials are highly correlated across occupations. At first blush it would be unlikely that the same reasons that cause firms in one industry to pay high wages to its machinists would cause them to pay high wages to janitors, or to cooks in the company cafeteria.

These correlations can be explained by a combination of efficiency wage considerations and psychological explanations. The argument is as follows. For efficiency wage reasons some workers receive compensation packages and amenities that give them high levels of job satisfaction; i.e. the utility level associated with the job is considerably above that needed to fill the job. One form these amenities could take is to have highly competent support personnel such as janitors or cafeteria workers. By offering high wages to support personnel the firm is likely to attract better workers to those jobs. (Here we are using the sorting version of the efficiency wage model). Of course, support personnel are still likely to be paid significantly less than workers whose wages are determined directly by efficiency wage considerations and who are more highly skilled. These wage differences may generate morale problems, causing poor performance by the support personnel which lowers the value of the job to the more highly paid workers. By paying support personnel higher wages than they would expect to receive elsewhere these morale problems would be mitigated.

Policy implications

Typically, the market equilibrium of these models will fail to be Pareto efficient, even in a second-best sense. There are government interventions that can improve the allocation of resources in the economy. Rather than delineating the entire package of taxes and subsidies that will be needed to effect Pareto improvements in these models, we can convey the spirit of these market imperfections and the proposed solutions by describing instead government policies that increase aggregate output.

In the adverse selection model, workers may be misassigned. Workers in the industrial sector may be ones with a comparative disadvantage in industrial employment relative to a randomly selected worker in the non-industrial sector. This misassignment occurs because firms cannot directly observe the reservation wages of workers. Because observationally identical workers are paid the same wage, firms will pay wages and hire types of workers that generate a relatively homogeneous labor force, even if those policies result in an inefficient allocation of labor among jobs. Government policies designed to lower or raise the wages paid by firms can increase aggregate output by inducing firms to hire workers with a comparative advantage in industrial employment when those workers would otherwise be unprofitable to the firm. These interventions in the labor market can take the form of direct policies such as minimum wage laws that induce firms to hire groups with higher reservation wages; or indirect policies such as per employee taxes or subsidies—in each case the tax or subsidy could be balanced by a countervailing payroll subsidy or tax that makes the government intervention revenue neutral. Since, in a sorting model, the payroll tax (subsidy) does not affect the wage the firm offers, the direction of the effect of the per employee subsidy (tax) would not be changed by a payroll tax (subsidy).

Other policies that could improve aggregate output would be measures to increase the information available to employers about performance in school and on previous jobs. This information would mitigate the informational imperfections that penalize workers who can not easily sort themselves. As a side benefit it would also improve performance in school and on jobs.

For the incentive model, one might consider direct subsidies to the industrial sector as a means of improving aggregate welfare. Although a full general equilibrium analysis of the effects of these policies has not been done, it seems likely that those policies would also increase income inequality and poverty (using the Atkinson or Sen measures).

For the Dasgupta–Ray nutrition model, we pointed out that land redistribution could both improve the distribution of income and increase aggregate output. These measures could very well have opposite effects in the effort model.

Indeed, as we have shown it is not uncommon for different efficiency wage models to have opposite policy implications. Consequently, one should be cautious about making policy recommendations. While it is clear that the market equilibrium is unlikely to maximize aggregate output, it is by no means clear whether any particular policy intervention will do more good than harm.

For example, throughout our analysis of efficiency wage models we assumed that labor inputs into production can be aggregated in terms of efficiency units. However, if the production process was such that it worked at the pace of the slowest worker as in the case of an assembly line, or if production required some highly skilled workers, that assumption would not be valid, and the results could change dramatically. In general, policies that increase the information available to firms seem most likely to be helpful. However, in general, the efficacy of government policy is likely to be sensitive to particular features of the economy or industry in question. Before formulating policy there is no substitute for a careful investigation of the technological and institutional features of the relevant markets.

104   ANDREW WEISS

References

Abraham, K. G. and Farber, H. S., (1987). "Job Duration, Seniority, and Earnings." *American Economic Review*, **77**, No. 3, 278–297.

Abraham, K. G. and Katz, L. F., (1986). "Cyclical Unemployment: Sectoral Shifts or Aggregate Disturbances?" *Journal of Political Economics*, **94**, No. 3, Part 7; 507–522.

Akerlof, G. and Katz, L. F., (1989). "Workers' Trust Funds and the Logic of Wage Profiles." *Quarterly Journal of Economics*, August 1989, 525–537.

Abreu, D., Milgrom, P. and Pearce, D., (1987). "Information and Timing in Repeated Partnerships." Harvard University, UC Berkeley and Yale University. (Unpublished paper).

Akerlof, G. A., (1970). "The Market for Lemons: Qualitative Uncertainty and the Market Mechanism." *Quarterly Journal of Economics*, **XXXIV**, No. 3, 488–500.

Akerlof, G. A., (1976). "The Economics of Caste and of the Rat Race and Other Woeful Tales." *Quarterly Journal of Economics*, **XL**, No. 4, 599–617.

Akerlof, G. A., (1980). "The Economics of Social Customs, of Which Unemployment May Be One Consequence." *Quarterly Journal of Economics*, **XLIV**, No. 4, 749–76.

Akerlof, G. A., (1982). "Labor Contracts as Partial Gift Exchange." *Quarterly Journal of Economics*, **XLVII**, No. 4, 543–69.

Akerlof, G. A., (1984). "Gift Exchange and Efficiency Wage Theory: Four Views." *American Economic Review*, Papers and Proceedings, **74**, No. 2, 79–83.

Akerlof, G. A. and Miyazaki, H., (1980). "The Implicit Contract Theory of Unemployment Meets the Wage Bill Argument," *Review of Economic Studies*, **47**(2):321–338.

Akerlof, G. A. and Yellen, J., (1985a). "A Near Rational Model of the Business Cycle, with Wage and Price Inertia." *Quarterly Journal of Economics*, **C**, Supplement, 823–838.

Akerlof, G. A. and Yellen, J., (1985b). "Can Small Deviation from Rationality Make a Significant Difference to Economic Equilibria?" *American Economic Review*, **75**, No. 4, 708–720.

Allen, F., (1981). "Control of Capital, Sharecropping, Ability and Information." Nuffield College, Oxford. (mimeo)

Allen, S., (1984). "Trade Unions, Absenteeism and Exit-Voice." *Industrial and Labor Relations Review*, **37**, No. 3, 331–345.

Allen, S. G., (1987). "Relative Wage Variability in the United States, 1860–1983." NBER Working Paper No. 2221.

Altonji, J. and Ham, J., (1985). "The Collective Impact of Sectoral Shocks on Aggregate Employment Fluctuations." (mimeo)

Altonji, J. and Shakotko, R., (1987). "Do Wages Rise With Job Seniority?" *Review of Economic Studies*, **54**, No. 179, 437–460.

Antel, J. J., (1985). "Costly Labor Contract Negotiation and the Labor Mobility of Young Men." *American Economic Review*, **75**, No. 5, 976–991.

Arnott, R. J., (1982). The Structure of Multi-Period Employment Contracts with Incomplete Insurance Markets. *Canadian Journal of Economics*, **XV**, No. 1, 51–76.

Arnott, R. and Stiglitz, J., (1985). "Labor Turnover, Wage Structures and Moral Hazard: The Inefficiency of Competitive Markets." *Journal of Labor Economics*, **3**, 434–462.

Azariadis, C., (1975). "Implicit Contracts and Underemployment Equilibria." *Journal of Political Economics*, **83**, 6, 1183-1202.

Baily, M. N., (1974). "Wage and Employment under Uncertain Demand." *The Review of Economic Studies*, **XLI** (1), No. 125, 37-50.

Beaudry, Paul, (1988). "Entry Wages Signalling Future Wages: Theory and Evidence on a Link between Turnover Costs and Job Rationing."

Becker, G. S. and Stigler, G. J., (1974). Law Enforcement, Malfeasance, and the Compensation of Enforcers. *Journal of Legal Studies*, 1-18.

Bell, L. and Freeman, R. B., (1985). "Does a Flexible Industry Wage Structure Increase Employment? The U.S. Experience." NBER Working Paper.

Bernanke, B. and Powell, J., (1985). "The Cyclical Behavior of Industrial Labor Markets: A Comparison of Pre-War and Post-War Eras." University of Bonn. (mimeo)

Benassy, J. P., (1975). "Neo-Keynesian Disequilibrium in a Monetary Economy." *Review of Economic Studies*, **XLII** (4), No. 132, 502-523.

Bhattacharya, S., (1983). "Tournaments and Incentives: Heterogeneity and Essentiality." Stanford University. (mimeo)

Bhattacharya, S., (1980). "Nondissipative Signalling Structures and Dividend Policy," *Quarterly Journal of Economics*, **XLV**, No. 1, 1-24.

Bils, M. J., (1985). "Real Wages Over the Business Cycle: Evidence from Panel Data." *Journal of Political Economy*, **93**, No. 4, 666-89.

Bils, M. J. (1988). "Rigid Wages and Employment Fluctuations When Past Variability Predicts Future Variability," University of Rochester working paper.

Bliss, C. J. and Stern, N. H., (1978a). "Productivity, Wages and Nutrition, 1: The Theory." *Journal of Development Economics*, **5**, 331-362.

Bliss, C. J. and Stern, N. H., (1978b). "Productivity, Wages and Nutrition, 2: Some Observations." *Journal of Development Economics*, **5**, 363-398.

Bloch, F. and Kuskin, M., (1978). "Wage Determination in the Union and Nonunion Sectors." *Industrial and Labor Relations Review*, **31**, No. 2, 183-92.

Bowles, S., (1985). "The Production Process in a Competitive Economy: Walrasian, Neo-Hobbesian and Marxian Models." *American Economic Review*, **75**, No. 1, 16-36.

Brown, G., (1985). "Standard-Rate Wage Setting, Labor Quality, and Unions." NBER Working Paper.

Brown, C. and Medoff, J., (1985). "The Employer Size-Wage Effect." NBER Working Paper.

Bowles, S., (1981). "Competitive Wage Determination and Involuntary Unemployment: A Conflict Model." University of Massachusetts. (mimeo)

Braverman, A. and Srinivasan, T. N., (1981). "Credit and Sharecropping in Agrarian Societies." *Journal of Development Economics*, **9**, No. 3, 289-312.

Braverman, A. and Stiglitz, J. E. (1982). "Sharecropping and the Interlinking of Agrarian Markets." *American Economic Review*, **72**, 695-715.

Braverman, A. and Stiglitz, J. E., (1985). "Landlords, Tenants and Technological Innovations." *Journal of Develoment Economics*.

Bryson, C. M. and Siddiqui, M. M., (1969). "Some Criteria for Aging." *Journal of the American Statistical Association*, **64**,1 472-1483.

Bulow, J. I. and Summers, L. H., (1986). "A Theory of Dual Labor Markets with Application to Industrial Policy, Discrimination and Keynesian Unemployment." *Journal of Labor Economics*, **4**, 376-415.

Butters, G. R., (1977). "Equilibrium Distributions of Sales and Advertising Prices." *Review of Economic Studies*, **XLIV** (3), No. 138, 465-491.

Cain, G., (1984). "The Economic Analysis of Labor Market Discrimination: A Survey." Institute for Research on Poverty Special Report No. 37.

Calvo, G., (1979). "Quasi-Walrasian Theories of Unemployment." *American Economic Review Proceedings*, **69**, No. 2, 102–7.

Calvo, G., (1985). "The Inefficiency of Unemployment: The Supervision Perspective." *Quarterly Journal of Economics*, **L** (2), 373–87.

Calvo, G. A. and Wellisz, S., (1978). "Supervision, Loss of Control, and the Optimum Size of the firm." *Journal of Political Economy*, **86**, No. 5, 943–52.

Calvo, G. A. and Wellisz, S., (1979). "Hierarchy, Ability and Income Distribution." *Journal of Political Economics*, Part 1. **87**, No. 5, 991–1010.

Carmichael, L., (1983). "Firm-specific Human Capital and Promotion Ladders." *Bell Journal of Economics*, **4**, No. 1, 251–58.

Carmichael, L., (1985). "Can Unemployment be Involuntary?: Comment." *American Economic Review*, **75**, No. 5, 1213–14.

Carmichael, L., (1987). "Efficiency Wage Models of Unemployment: A Survey," Working Paper, Queen's University.

Cheung, S. N. S., (1969). *The Theory of Share Tenancy*. Chicago: University of Chicago Press.

Clemenz, G., (1985). "The Impact of Imperfect Monitoring on the Efficiency Wage Hypothesis." Presented at the annual meeting of the Austrian Economic Association.

Clemenz, G., (1986). *Credit Markets with Asymmetric Information*, Berlin: Springer-Verlag.

Coleman, T., (1987). "Unemployment Behavior: Evidence from the CPS Work Experience Survey," State University of New York at Stony Brook Working Paper.

Cooper, R., (1983). "A Note on Overemployment/Underemployment in Labor Contracts Under Asymmetric Information." *Economics Letters*, **12**, No. 1, 81–87.

Cooper, R., (1987). *Wage and Employment Patterns in Labor Contracts: Micro-foundations and Macro-economic Implications*. Harvard Academic Publishers.

Cullen, D., (1956). "The Interindustry Wage Structure, 1899–1950," *American Economic Review*, **XLVI**, No. 3, 353–369.

Cuny, C., (1986). "Uniform Wages and Involuntary Unemployment with Rish-Adverse Workers." mimeo, Graduate School of Business, Stanford University.

Dasgupta, P. and Ray, D., (1984). "Inequality, Malnutrition and Unemployment: A Critique of the Competitive Market Mechanism," IMSSS Technical Report No. 454.

Dasgupta, P. and Ray, D., (1985). "Inequality, Malnutrition and Unemployment: A Critique of the Competitive Market Mechanism," Working Paper, University of Cambridge and Stanford University.

Dasgupta, P. and Ray, D., (1986). "Inequality as a Determinant of Malnutrition and Unemployment: Theory." *Economic Journal*, **96**(384), 1011–34.

Dasgupta, P. and Ray, D., (1987). "Inequality as a Determinant of Malnutrition and Unemployment: Policy." *Economic Journal*, **97**(385), 177–88.

Dickens, W. T., (1986). "Wages, Employment and the Threat of Collective Action by Workers." (mimeo)

Dickens, W. T. and Katz, L. F., (1986). "Industry Wage Patterns and Theories of Wage Determination." U.C. Berkeley. (mimeo)

Dickens, W. L. and Katz, L., (1987). "Inter Industry Wage Differences and Industry Characteristics." *Unemployment and the Structure of Labor Markets*. (K. Lang and J. S. Leonard, ed.) Oxford: Basil Blackwell.

Dickens, W. T., Katz, L. F., and Lang, K., (1986). "Are Efficiency Wages Efficient?" (mimeo).

Dickens, W. T., Katz, L. F., Lang, K. and Summers, L., (1989). "Employee Crime and the Monitoring Puzzle." *Journal of Labor Economics*, 7, 331-347.

Dickens, W. T. and Lang, K., (1985). "A Test of Dual Labor Market Theory." *American Economic Review*, 75, No. 4, 792-805.

Dickens, W. T. and Lang, K., (1985). "Testing Dual Labor Market Theory: A Reconsideration of the Evidence." NBER Working Paper #1670.

Dutta, P. K. and Radner, R., (1987). "Principal-Agent Games in Continuous Time," Working Paper, AT&T Bell Laboratories.

Doeringer, P. B. and Piore, M. J., (1971). *Internal Labor Markets and Manpower Analysis*. D. C. Heath, Lexington, Mass.

Dunlop, J., (1985). "Industrial Relations and Economics: The Common Frontier of Wage Determination." *IRRA Proceedings 1984*.

Dybvig, P. and Jaynes, C., (1980). "Output-supply, Employment and Intra-Industry Wage Dispersion." Cowles Foundation Discussion Paper No. 546.

Eaton, B. C., (1983). "The Economy of High Wages: An Agency Problem." *Economica*, 50, No. 198, 175-81.

Eaton, B. C. and Neher, P. A., (1985). "Unemployment, Underemployment, and Optimal Job Search." *Journal of Political Economy*, 355-375.

Eaton, B. C. and White, W., (1982). "Agent Compensation and the Limits of Bonding." *Economic Inquiry*, XX, No. 3, 330-343.

Ehrenberg, R. G., (1971). "Heterogeneous Labor, The Internal Labor Market, and the Dynamics of the Employment-Hours Decision." *Journal of Economic Theory*, 3, No. 1, 85-104.

F. A. O., (1957). *Calorie Requirements*. Rome. Nutritional Studies.

F. A. O., (1962). *Nutrition and Working Efficiency*. Rome. Freedom from Hunger Campaign Basic Study.

F. A. O., (1963). *Third World Food Survey*, Rome. Freedom from Hunger Campaign Basic Study.

F. A. O., (1973). *Energy and Protein Requirements*. Rome. Nutrition Meetings Report.

F. A. O., (1974). *Assessment of the World Food Situation, Present and Future*. United Nations, World Food Conference (Item 8 of the Provisional Agenda).

Fei, J. C. H. and Chiang, A. C., (1966). "Maximum-Speed Development Through Austerity. *The Theory and Design of Economic Development."* (I. Adelman and E. Thorbecke, eds) Baltimore: Johns Hopkins University Press.

Fields, G., (1975). "Rural-Urban Migration, Urban Unemployment and Underemployment, and Job-Search Activity in LDC." *Journal of Development Economics*, 2, No. 2, 165-187.

Foster, J. E. and Wan, Jr., H. Y., (1984). "Involuntary Underemployment as a Principal-Agent Equilibrium." *American Economic Review*, 74, No. 3, 476-484.

Foulkens, F., (1980). *Personnel Policies in Large Nonunion Companies*. Prentice-Hall, Englewood Cliffs, NJ.

Freeman, R. B., (1980). "The Exit-Voice Tradeoff in the Labor Market, Unionism, Job Tenure, Quits and Separations." *Quarterly Journal of Economics*, XLIV, No. 4, 643-73.

Freeman, R. B., (1981). "The Effect of Trade Unionism on Fringe Benefits." *Industrial and Labor Relations Review*, 34, No. 4, 489-509.

Freeman, R. B., (1983). "Unionism, Price-Cost Margins and the Return to Capital." Harvard University. (mimeo)

Freeman, R. B. and Medoff, J., (1981). "The Impact of Collective Bargaining: Illusion or Reality?" *U.S. Industrial Relations 1950-1980: A Critical Assessment*. (J. Stieber, R. B. McKersie and D. Q. Mills, eds) IRRA, Madison, WI.

Freeman, R. B. and Medoff, J., (1984). "What Do Unions Do?" New York: Basic Books.

Futia, C., (1977). "Excess Supply Equilibria." *Journal of Economic Theory*, **14**, 200–220.

Gintis, H. and Ishikawa, T., (1983). "Wages, Work Discipline and Macroeconomic Equilibrium." (mimeo)

Gintis, H. and Ishikawa, T., (1985). "The Theory of Production and Price in Recontracting Markets." (unpublished paper). University of Massachusetts and University of Tokyo.

Goldin, C., (1986). "Monitoring Costs and Occupational Segregation by Sex: A Historical Analysis." *Journal of Labor Economics*, **4**, No. 1, 1–27.

Gordon, D. F., (1974). "A Neo-Classical Theory of Keynesian Unemployment." *Economics Industry*, **12**(4), 431–59.

Green, J. and Kahn, C., (1974). "Wage Employment Contracts." *Quarterly Journal of Economics*, 173–87.

Green, J. and Stokey, N., (1983). "A Comparison of Tournaments and Contests." *Journal of Political Economy*, **91**, No. 3, 349–364.

Greenwald, B. C. N., (1979). *Adverse Selection in the Labor Market*, Garland, New York: London.

Greenwald, B. C. N., (1986). "Adverse Selection in the Labor Market." *Review of Economic Studies*, **LIII**, 325–347.

Gronau, R., (1971). "Information and Frictional Unemployment." *American Economic Review*, **LXI**, No. 3, Part I, 290–301.

Grossman, H., (1978). "Risk Shifting, Layoffs, and Seniority." *Journal of Monetary Economics*, **4**, No. 4, 661–686.

Grossman, H. I., (1979). "Adverse Selection, Dissembling, and Competitive Equilibrium." *Bell Journal of Economics*, **10**, No. 1, 336–343.

Grossman, S. J. and Hart, O. D., (1981). "Implicit Contracts, Moral Hazard and Unemployment." *American Economic Review Proceedings*, **71**, No. 2, 301–307.

Grossman, S. J. and Hart, O. D., (1981). "An Analysis of the Principal-Agent Problem." *Econometrica*, **51**, No. 1, 7–45.

Grossman, S., Hart, O., and Maskin, E., (1983). "Observable Aggregate Shocks with Unobservable Consequences." *Journal of Political Economy*, **91**, No. 6, 907–928.

Groves, T. F., (1973). "Incentives in Teams." *Econometrica*, **41**, No. 4, 617–631.

Guasch, J. A., (1981). "Test Characteristics, Precision Differences and Labor Market Allocations." University of California, San Diego. Discussion Paper No. 13.

Guasch, J. L. and Weiss, A., (1980a). "Wages as Sorting Mechanisms in Competitive Markets with Asymmetric Information: A Theory of Testing." *Review of Economic Studies*, **XCIV**, No. 3, 149–165.

Guasch, J. L. and Weiss, A., (1980b). "Adverse Selection by Markets and the Advantage of Being Late." *Quarterly Journal of Economics*, **94**, 453–466.

Guasch, J. L. and Weiss, A., (1981). "Self-Selection in the Labor Market." *American Economic Review*, **71**, 275–284.

Guasch, J. L. and Weiss, A., (1982). "An Equilibrium Analysis of Wage-Productivity Gaps." *Review of Economic Studies*, **XLIX** (4), No. 158, 485–497.

Hall, R. E., (1970). "Why Is the Unemployment Rate So High at Full Employment?" *Brookings Papers*, 369–402. Washington.

Hall, R. E., (1975). "The Rigidity of Wages and the Persistence of Unemployment." *Brookings Papers on Economic Activity*, 301–335.

Hall, R. E., (1980). "Employment Fluctuations and Wage Rigidity." *Brookings Papers on Economic Activity*, 91–132.

Hammermesh, D., (1977). "Economic Aspects of Job Satisfaction." *Essays in Labor Market Analysis*. (O. Ashenfelter and W. Oates, eds) New York: Halstead Press.

Hammermesh, D. and Goldfarb, R. S., (1970). "Manager Programs in a Local Labor

Market: A Theoretical Note." *American Economic Review*, **LX**, No. 4, 706-709.
Harris, J. R. and Todaro, M. P., (1970). "Migration, Unemployment, and Development: A Two-Sector Analysis." *American Economic Review*, **LX**, No. 1, 126-143.
Hart, O. D., (1983). "Optimal Labor Contracts Under Asymmetric Information: An Introduction." *Review of Economic Studies*, **L** (1), No. 160, 3-35.
Hellwig, M., (1985). "Modelling Competition in Markets with Adverse Selection." Bonn. Paper presented at the Workshop on Information, Incentives, and Strategic Behavior.
Hodson, R. and England, P., (1985). "Industrial Structure and Sex Differences in Earnings." (mimeo)
Holmstrom, B., (1979). "Moral Hazard and Observality." *Bell Journal of Economics*, **10**, No. 1, 74-91.
Holmstrom, B., (1982). "Moral Hazard in Teams." *Bell Journal of Economics*, **13**, No. 2, 324-340.
Holmstrom, B., (1983). "Equilibrium Long-Term Labor Contracts." *Quarterly Journal of Economics*, 23-54. Supplement.
Hurwicz, L. and Shapiro, L. (1978). "Incentive Structure Maximizing Residual Gain Under Incomplete Information." *Bell Journal of Economics*, **9**, No. 1, 180-91.
Ippolito, R. A., (1985). "The Labor Government and True Economic Pension Liabilities." *American Economic Review*, **75**, No. 5, 1031-1043.
Jacoby, S., (1983). "Industrial Mobility in Historical Perspective." *Industrial Relations*, 261-282.
Johnson, G. E. and Layard, P. R. G., "The Natural Rate of Employment: Explanation and Policy," in *Handbook of Labor Economics* (O. Ashenfelter and R. Layard, eds), Vol. II, Elsevier Science Publishers BV, pp. 921-999.
Jones, S. R. G., (1985). "Dual Labor Markets, Productivity and Unemployment." University of British Columbia. (mimeo)
Jovanovic, B., (1979). "Job Matching and the Theory of Turnover." *Journal of Political Economy*, **87**, 972-90.
Katz, L., (1986). "Efficiency Wage Theories: A Partial Evaluation." *National Bureau of Economic Research Macroeconomics Annual*, 235-276.
Keeton, William R., (1979). *Equilibrium Credit Rationing*. New York: Garland Publishing.
Keynes, John M., (1936). *The Central Theory of Employment Interest and Money*. New York.
Kreps, D. M., (1984). "Corporate Culture and Economic Theory." Stanford Graduate School of Business, Mimeo.
Kreps, D. M., (1985). "Signalling Games and Stable Equilibria." Stanford Graduate School of Business. (mimeo)
Kreps, D. M. and Ramey, G., (1986). "Structural Consistency and Sequential Rationality." Technical Report No. 488, Stanford University.
Kreps, D. M. and Wilson, R. B., (1982). "Sequential Equilibria." *Econometrica*, **50**, No. 4, 863-894.
Krueger, A. B., (1989). "Ownership, Agency and Wages: An Examination of Franchising in the Fast Food Industry." Princeton University Working Paper.
Krueger, A. B. and Summers, L. H., (1988). "Efficiency Wages and the Inter-Industry Wage Structure." *Econometrica*, **56**, No. 2, 259-294.
Krueger, A. B. and Summers, L. H., (1987). "Reflections on the Interindustry Wage Structure." *Unemployment and the Structure of Labor Markets*, (Kevin Lang and J. S. Leonard, eds) Oxford: Basil Blackwell.
Kwoka, J., (1983). "Monopoly, Plant, and Union Effects on Worker Wages." *Industrial and Labor Reflections Review*, **36**, No. 2, 251-257.

Lang, K., Leonard, J. and Lilien, D. A., (1987). "Labor Market Structure, Wages and Unemployment." *Unemployment and the Structure of Labor Markets*, (Kevin Lang and J. S. Leonard, eds) Oxford: Basil Blackwell.

Landau, H. and Weiss, A., (1985). "Wage Hiring Standards and Firm Size." *Journal of Labor Economics*, **2**, No. 4, 477-499.

Lawrence, C. and Lawrence, R., (1985). "Relative Wages in U.S. Manufacturing: An Endgame Interpretation." *Brookings Papers on Economic Activity*, 47-106.

Lazear, E., (1979). "Why Is There Mandatory Retirement?" *Journal of Political Economy*, **87**, No. 6, 1261-1284.

Lazear, E. P., (1981). "Agency, Earnings Profiles, Productivity, and Hours Restrictions." *American Economic Review*, 606-20.

Lazear, E., (1983). "Salaries and Piece Rates." NORC Working Paper No. 83-15.

Lazear, E. P., (1987). "Job Security and Unemployment." University of Chicago. (unpublished paper)

Lazear, E. and Moore, R., (1984). "Incentives, Productivity and Labor Contracts." *Quarterly Journal of Economics*, May 1984, 275-296.

Lazear, E. P. and Rosen, S., (1981). "Rank-Order Tournaments as Optimal Labor Contracts." *Journal of Political Economy*, **89**, 841-864.

Leibenstein, H., (1957). *Economic Backwardness and Economic Growth*. New York: Wiley.

Levine, D., (1986). "Tests of Efficiency Wage and Bargaining Theories: The Pay Productivity Relation." Harvard University. (mimeo)

Lewis, E., (1960). "Incentive Wage Payment in Manufacturing." *Monthly Labor Review*, 190-193.

Lewis, H. G., (1983). "Union Relative Wage Effects: A Survey of Macro Estimates." *Journal of Labor Economics*, **1**, No. 1, 1-27.

Li, E., (1986). "Compensating Differentials for Cyclical and Noncyclical Unemployment." *Journal of Labor Economics*, **4**, No. 2, 277-300.

Lilien, D., (1982). "Sectoral Shifts and Cyclical Unemployment." *Journal of Political Economy*, **90**, No. 4, 777-793.

Lindbeck, A. and Snower, D. J., (1984a). "Involuntary Unemployment as an Insider-Outsider Dilemma." Institute for International Economic Studies, University of Stockholm, Seminar Paper No. 282.

Lindbeck, A. and Snower, D. J., (1984b). "Labor Turnover, Insider Morale and Involuntary Unemployment." Institute for International Economic Studies, University of Stockholm, Seminar Paper No. 310.

Lindbeck, A. and Snower, D. J., (1986). "Wage Setting, Unemployment and Insider-Outsider Relations." *American Economic Review*, **76**(2):235-239.

Lindbeck, A. and Snower, D. J., (1987a). "Union Activity, Unemployment Persistence and Wage-Employment Ratchets," *European Economic Review*, **31**(1-2):157-167.

Lindbeck, A. and Snower, D. J., (1987b). "Efficiency Wages Versus Insiders and Outsiders," *European Economic Review*, **31**(1-2):407-416.

Lindbeck, A. and Snower, D. J., (1988). "Cooperation, Harassment and Involuntary Unemployment—An Insider—Outsider Approach," *American Economic Review*, **78**(1):167-188.

Lippman, S. and McCall, J. J., (1976). "The Economics of Job Search: A Survey." *Economic Inquiry*, **XIV**, No. 2, 155-189.

Long, J. E. and Link, A. N. (1983). "The Impact of Market Structure on Wages, Fringe Benefits, and Turnover," *Industrial and Labor Relations Review*, **36**, No. 2, 239-250.

Lucas, R. E. and Prescott, E. C., (1974). "Equilibrium Search and Unemployment." *Journal of Economic Theory*, **7**, 188-209.

MacDonald, G., (1982). "A Market Equilibrium Theory of Job Assignment and Sequential Accumulation of Information." *American Economic Review*, **72**, 1038-1055.

Malcomson, J., (1981). "Unemployment and the Efficiency Wage Hypothesis." *Economic Journal*, **91**, No. 364, 848-866.

Malcomson, J., (1984). "Work Incentives, Hierarchy, and Internal Labor Markets." *Journal of Political Economy*, **92**, No. 3, 486-507.

Malinvaud, E., (1977). *Theory of Unemployment Reconsidered*, Basil Blackwell, Oxford.

Mankiw, N. G., (1985). "Small Menu Costs and Large Business Cycles: A Macro-economic Model of Monopoly." *Quarterly Journal of Economics*, **C** (2), 529-538.

Marshall, J. M., (1976). "Moral Hazard." *American Economic Review*, **66**, No. 5, 880-890.

Marshall, J., (1983). "An Equilibrium Model of Search and Non-Price Rationing." University of California, Santa Barbara, Economics Department, Santa Barbara. Working Paper No. 231.

Marshall, R. C. and Zarkin, G. A., (1987). "The Effect of Job Tenure on Wage Offers," *Journal of Labor Economics*, **5**(3), 301-24.

McDonald, I. M. and Solow, R. M., (1981). "Wage Bargaining and Employment." *American Economic Review*, **71**, No. 5, 896-908.

Medoff, J. L. and Abraham, K. G., (1980). "Experience, Performance and Earnings." *Quarterly Journal of Economics*, **XCV**, No. 4, 703-36.

Medoff, J. L. and Abraham, K. G., (1981). "Are Those Paid More Really More Productive? The Case of Experience." *Journal Of Human Resources*, **16**, 186-216.

Mellow, W., (1982). "Employer Size and Wages." *Review of Economics and Statistics*, **LXIV**, No. 3, 495-501.

Milkovich, G. and Newman, J., (1981). *Compensation*. Business Publications, Inc., Plano, Texas.

Miller, R. A., (1984). "Job Matching and Occupational Choice." *Journal of Political Economy*, **92**, 1086-1120.

Mirrless, J. A., (1975). "A Pure Theory of Underdeveloped Economics." *Agriculture in Development Theory*, (L. Reynolds, ed.) New Haven, Connecticut: Yale University Press.

Mirrless, J., (1976). "The Optimal Structure of Incentives and Authority within an Organization." *Bell Journal of Economics*, **7**, No. 1, 105-31.

Miyazaki, H., (1984). "Work Norms and Involuntary Unemployment." *Quarterly Journal of Economics*, **XCIX**, No. 2, 297-312.

Moffitt, R., Keane, M. and Runkle, D., (1987). "Real Wages Over the Business Cycle: Estimating the Impact of Heterogeneity with Micro Data," Brown University Working Paper.

Montgomery, E. and Stockton, D., (1985). "Evidence on Causes of the Rising Dispersion of Relative Wages." (mimeo)

Mookherjee, D., (1984a). "Involuntary Unemployment and Worker Self-Selection." Graduate School of Business, Stanford University, Research Paper #741.

Mookherjee, D., (1984b). "Involuntary Unemployment and Worker Moral Hazard." Graduate School of Business, Stanford University, Research Paper #745.

Mookherjee, D., (1986). "Involuntary Unemployment and Worker Moral Hazard." *Rev. Econ. Stud.* **53**: 739-754.

Mookherjee, Dilip, (1988). "Involuntary Unemployment and Worker Self-Selection." *Journal of Economic Theory*, **45**: 171-1888.

Murphy, K. M. and Topel, R., (1987). "Unemployment, Risk, and Earnings: Testing for

Equalizing Wage Differences in the Labor Market." *Unemployment and the Structure of Labor Markets.* (Kevin Land and J. S. Leonard, eds). Basil Blackwell, Oxford.

Nageshi, T., (1974). "Involuntary Unemployment and Market Imperfections," *Economic Studies Quarterly*, **25**, 32–41.

Nalebuff, B. and Stiglitz, J. E., (1985). "Price and Quality." (Unpublished mimeo)

Nalebuff, B. and Stiglitz, J. E., (1982). "Prices and Queues as Screening Devices in Competitive Markets." (Unpublished paper)

Nalebuff, B. and Stiglitz, J. E., (1983). "Prizes and Contests: Towards a General Theory of Compensation and Competition." *Bell Journal*, **14**, No. 1, 21–43.

Nalebuff, B., Stiglitz, J. E. and Negishi, T., (1979). "Quality and Prices." *Microeconomic Foundations of Keynesian Macroeconomics.* North Holland, Amsterdam.

Newbery, D. and Stiglitz, J. E., (1979). "Sharecropping, Risk Sharing and the Importance of Imperfect Information." *Risk, Uncertainty and Development.* (J. A. Roumasset, J. M. Boussard and I. Singh, eds). 311–341. SEARCA, A/D/C.

Ohashi, I., (1985). "Cyclical Variations in Wage Differentials and Unemployment." Nagoya City University Working Paper.

Oi, W., (1983). "Heterogeneous Firms and the Organization of Production." *Economic Inquiry*, **XXI**, No. 2, 147–71.

Okun, A., (1973). "Upward Mobility in a High-Pressure Economy." *Brookings Papers on Economic Activity*, 207–52.

Okun, A., (1982). "Prices and Quantities: A Macro-economic Analysis." Brookings Institution.

Parsons, D. O., "Models of Labor Turnover, a Theoretical and Empirical Survey." In R. Ehrenberg, ed., *Research in Labor Economics.* Greenwich, Conn.; JAI Press, vol. 1, (1977): 185–225.

Parsons, D. O., "The Employment Relationship: Job Attachment, Work Effort, and the Nature of Contracts," in Ashenfelter O. and Layard R. (eds) *Handbook of Labor Economics* 1986.

Pascual, C. R. *et al.*, (1976). "Nutritional Requirements: Dietary Allowances and Requirements for Calories and Nutrients." *Food Consumption and Planning.* (K. K. P. N. Rao, ed.) Pergamon Press, New York.

Pencavel, J., (1970). *An Analysis of the Quit Rate in America Manufacturing Industry.* IR Section Princeton, Princeton, NJ.

Pencavel, J., (1977a). "Work, Effort, On-the-Job Screening and Alternative Method of Remuneration." *Research in Labor Economics.* (R. Ehrenberg, ed.) Greenwich, CT.: JAI Press.

Pencavel, J., (1977b). "Industrial Morale." *Essays in Labor Market Analysis*: (O. Ashenfelter and W. Oates, eds) New York: Halstead Press.

Phelps, Edmund *et al.*, (1970a). *The Microeconomic Foundations of Employment and Inflation Theory.* New York.

Phelps, Edmund *et al.*, (1970b). "Money Wage Dynamics and Labor Market Equilibrium." *The Microeconomic Foundations of Employment and Inflation Theory.* New York.

Pisauro, Giuseppe, "The Effect of Taxes on Labor in Efficiency Wage Models." *Journal of Public Economics* (submitted) 1989.

Pissarides, C., (1983). "Efficient Employment with Endogenous Jobs and Job Rejection." London School of Economics, London. Working paper.

Poterba, J. and Summers, L. H., (1984). "Adjusting the Gross Changes Data: Implications for Labor Market Dynamics." NBER Working Paper No. 1436.

Pugel, T., (1980). "Profitability, Concentration and the Interindustry Variation in Wages." *Review of Economics and Statistics.* **XIII**, No. 2, 248–53.

Radner, R., (1981). "Monitoring Cooperative Agreements in a Repeated Principal-Agent Relationship." *Econometrica*, **49**, No. 5, 1127–1148.

Radner, R., (1985). "Repeated-Agent Games with Discounting." *Econometrica*, **53**, No. 5, 1173–1198.

Rao, V., (1982). *Food, Nutrition and Poverty in India*. Delhi: Vikas Publishing House.

Read, M. S., (1977). "Malnutrition and Human Performance." *Malnutrition, Behavior and Social Organization*. (L. S. Green, ed.) New York: Academic Press.

Reder, M., (1962). "Wage Differentials: Theory and Management." *Aspects of Labor Economics*. Universities-NBER, Princeton, NJ: Princeton U. Press.

Reynolds, L. (1978). *Labor Economics and Labor Relations*, 7th Edition. Englewood Cliffs, NJ: Prentice-Hall.

Riordan, M. and Staiger, R. W., (1987). Sectoral Shocks and Structural Unemployment. Stanford University. (unpublished paper)

Rodgers, G., (1975). "Nutritionally Based Wage Determination in the Low Income Labor Market." *Oxford Economic Papers*, 61–81.

Rogerson, W. P., (1983). Repeated Moral Hazard. Economics Department, Stanford University, Stanford, CA. (Unpublished).

Rosen, S., (1983). Unemployment and Insurance. National Bureau of Economic Research, Working Paper No. 1095.

Rosen, S. (1985). The Theory of Equalizing Differences. NORC Discussion Paper No. 85-3.

Ross, S., (1973). The Economic Theory of Agency: The Principal's Problem. *American Economic Review*, Vol. LXIII, No. 2, 134–139

Rosenthal, R. W. and Weiss, A., (1984). Mixed-Strategy Equilibrium in a Market with Asymmetric Information. *Review of Economic Studies* 51, No 165, 333–342.

Rothschild, M. and Stiglitz, J. E., (1970). Increasing Risk I. A definition. *Journal of Economic Theory* 2, 225–243.

Rothschild, M. and Stiglitz J. E., (1971). Increasing Risk II. Its Economic Consequences. *Journal of Economic Theory* 3 (1) 66–84.

Rothschild, M. and Stiglitz, J. E., (1976). Equilibrium in Competitive Insurance Markets: An Essay on the Economics of Imperfect Information. *The Quarterly Journal of Economics*, Vol. XC (4) 629–50.

Ruback, R. and Zimmerman, M., (1984). Unionization and Profitability: Evidence from the Capital Market. *Journal of Political Economy*, Vol. 92, No. 6, 1134–57.

Rubinstein, A., (1979). Offenses that May Have Been Committed by Accident — An Optimal Policy of Retribution. *Applied Game Theory*. (S. J. Brams et al., ed) Physica-Verlag, Wurzburg.

Sah, R. K. and Stiglitz, J. E., (1985). The Social Cost of Labor and Project Evaluation: A General Approach. *Journal of Public Economics*, 28(2):135–163.

Salop, S. C., (1973a). Systematic Job Search and Unemployment. *Review of Economic Studies*, Vol. XL(2), No. 122, 191–201.

Salop, S. C., (1973b). Wage Differentials in a Dynamic Theory of the Firm. *Journal of Economic Theory*, Vol. 6, No. 4, 321–44.

Salop, S. C., (1978). Monopolistic Competition with Outside Goods. University of Pennsylvania, (unpublished paper).

Salop, S. C., (1979), A Model of Natural Rate of Unemployment. *American Economic Review*, Vol. 69, No. 1, 117–125.

Salop, J. K. and Salop, S. C., (1976). Self-Selection and Turnover in the Labor Market. *Quarterly Journal of Economics*, Vol. XC, No. 4, 619–27.

Sargent, T. J., (1979). *Macroeconomic Theory*. New York: Academic Press.

Schlict, E., (1975). "Labor Turnover, Wage Structural and Natural Unemployment." *Zeitschrift fur die Gesamte Staatswissenschaft* 89, **134**, 337–46. Academic Press, New York.

Selten, R., (1975). "A Re-examination of the Perfectness Concept for Equilibrium
Points in Extensive Games." *International Journal of Game Theory*, 25–55.
Shaked, A. and Sutton, J., (1984). "Involuntary Unemployment as a Perfect Equili-
brium in a Bargaining Model." *Econometrica*, 52, No. 6, 1351–1364.
Shapiro, C. and Stiglitz, J. E., (1984). "Equilibrium Unemployment as a Worker
Discipline Device." *American Economic Review*, 74, No. 3, 433–444.
Shapiro, C. and Stiglitz, J. E., (1985). "Can Unemployment be Involuntary: Reply."
American Economic Review, 75, No. 5, 1215–1217.
Slichter, S., (1950). "Notes on the Structure of Wages." *Review of Economics and
Statistics*, XXXIII, No. 1, 80–91.
Snower, D. J., (1983a). "Imperfect Competition, Underemployment and Crowding-
Out." *Oxford Economic Papers* (Supplement), 35, 245–70.
Snower, D. J., (1983b). "Search, Flexible Wages and Involuntary Unemployment."
Birkbeck College, University of London, Discussion Paper No. 132.
Solow, R., (1979a). "Alternative Approaches to Macroeconomic Theory: A Partial
View." *Canadian Journal of Economics*, 12, 339–354.
Solow, R., (1979b). "Another Possible Source of Wage Stickness." *Journal of Macro-
economics*, 1, No. 1, 79–82.
Solow, R., (1980). "On Theories of Unemployment." *American Economic Review*, 70,
No. 1, 1–10.
Solow, R., (1985). "Insiders and Outsiders in Wage Determination." *Scandinavian
Journal of Economic*, 87, 411–28.
Soskice, D., (1974). "Salop and Stiglitz on Involuntary Unemployment." University of
California-Berkeley. (unpublished paper)
Sparks, R. W., (1982). "A Model of Unemployment and Wage Rigidity." University of
California-Davis, (unpublished paper).
Stiglitz, J. E., (1974a). "Equilibrium Wage Distribution." Stanford University, IMMSS
Technical Report No. 154.
Stiglitz, J. E., (1974b). "Alternative Theories of Wage Determination and Unemploy-
ment in LDC's: The Labor Turnover Model," *Quarterly Journal of Economics*,
LXXXVIII, No. 2, 194–227.
Stiglitz, J. E., (1974c). "Incentives and Risk Sharing in Sharecropping." *Review of
Economic Studies*, 41, 219–255.
Stiglitz, J. E., (1975a). "Information and Economic Analysis." *Current Economic
Problems*. (M. Parkin and A. R. Nobay, eds) 27–52. Cambridge University Press,
Cambridge.
Stiglitz, J. E., (1975b). "An Economic Analysis of Labor Turnover." Stanford
University, Institute for Mathematical Studies in the Social Sciences, Stanford, CA.
Working Paper No. 53.
Stiglitz, J. E., (1975c). "Incentives, Risk and Information: Notes Towards a Theory of
Hierarchy." *Bell Journal of Economics and Management Science*, 6, 552–279.
Stiglitz, J. E., (1976). "The Efficiency Wage Hypothesis, Surplus Labor, and the
Distribution of Income in L.D.C.s." *Oxford Economic Papers*, 28, 185–207.
Stiglitz, J. E., (1982). *The Theory and Experience of Economic Development's Essays in
Honor of Sir W. Arthur Lewis*. (M. Gersovitz et al., eds) 78–106. G. Allen and
Unwin, London.
Stiglitz, J. E., (1983). "Risk, Incentives, and the Pure Theory of Moral Hazard." *The
Geneva Papers on Risk and Insurance*, 4–33.
Stiglitz, J. E., (1984). "Theories of Wage Rigidity." NBER, Cambridge, MA. NBER
Working Paper No. 1441.
Stiglitz, J. E. and Weiss, A., (1981). "Credit Rationing in Markets with Imperfect
Information." *American Economic Review*, 71, No. 3, 393–410.
Stiglitz, J. E. and Weiss, A., (1983). "Incentive Effects of Terminations: Applications to

the Credit and Labor Markets." *American Economic Review*, **73**, No. 5, 912–27.

Stiglitz, J. E. and Weiss, A., (1989). "Sorting Out the Difference Between Signaling and Screening Models." *Papers in Commemoration of the Economic Theory Seminar at Oxford University*; ed. Michael Dempster, Oxford University Press.

Stoft, Steven (1982). "Cheat-Threat Theory." University of California, Berkeley, Unpublished Ph.D. thesis.

Strand, J., (1985). "Unemployment as a Discipline Device Under Business Fluctuations." University of Oslo. (mimeo).

Taylor, J., (1982). "The Role of Expectations in the Choice of Monetary Policy." NBER Working Paper No. 1044.

Todaro, M., (1968). "An Analysis of Industrialization, Employment and Unemployment in Less Developed Countries." *Yale Economic Essays*, **8**, 331–402.

Topel, R. and Weiss, L., (1985). "Sectoral Uncertainty and Unemployment." UCLA Department of Economics Working Paper No. 384.

Vroman, W., (1978). "Cyclical Earnings Changes of Low Wage Workers." *Research in Labor Economics*. (R. Ehrenberg, ed.) Greenwich, CT: JAI Press.

Weiss, A., (1976). "A Theory of Limited Labor Markets." Stanford University, Unpublished Ph.D. Dissertation.

Weiss, A., (1980). "Job Queues and Layoffs in Labor Markets with Flexible Wages." *Journal of Political Economy*, **88**, No. 3, 526–38.

Weiss, A., (1983). "A Sorting-Cum-Learning Model of Education." *Journal of Political Economy*, **91**, No. 3; 420–442.

Weiss, A., (1985). "Wages and Absenteeism." *Economics Letters*, **19**, 277–279.

Weiss, A., (1988). "High School Graduation, Wage and Performance." *Journal of Political Economics*, **96**, No. 4, 785–820.

Weiss, A. and Landau, H. J., (1984). "A Theory of Wages, Hiring Standards and Firm Size." *Journal of Labor Economics*, **2**, 477–499.

Weiss, L., (1966). "Concentration and Labor Earnings." *American Economic Review*, **LVI**, No. 1, 96–117.

Weisskopf, T., Bowles, S. and Gordon, D., (1983). "Hearts and Minds: A Social Model of Aggregate Productivity Growth in the U.S., 1948–1979." *Brookings Papers on Economic Activity*, 381–441.

Weitzman, M. L., (1982). "Increasing Returns and the Foundations of Unemployment Theory." *Economic Journal*, **92**, No. 368, 787–804.

Williamson, O. E., Washter, M. L. and Harris, J. E., (1975). "Understanding the Employment Relation: The Analysis of Idiosyncratic Exchange." *Bell Journal of Economics*, **6**, No. 1, 250–78.

Wilson, C., (1979). "Equilibrium and Adverse Selection." *American Economic Review Proc.*, **69**, No. 2, 313–317.

Wilson, C., (1980a). "The Nature of Equilibrium in Markets with Adverse Selection." *Bell Journal of Economics*, **11**, No. 1, 108–30.

Wilson, C., (1980b). "A Model of Job-Search and Matching." University of Wisconsin, Economics Department, Madison. Working paper.

Wing, R., (1984). "Achieving Internal Equity Through Job Measurement." *Handbook of Wage and Salary Administration*. (M. Rock, ed.) New York: McGraw-Hill.

Woodbury, S. A. and Spiegelman, R. G., "Bonuses to Workers and Employers to Reduce Unemployment: Randomized trials in Illinois." *American Economic Review*, **77** (September 1987): 512–30.

Yellen, J., (1984). "Efficiency Wage Models of Unemployment." *American Economic Review*, **74**, No. 2, 200–208.

INDEX